Praise

"Dr. Stella integrates cutting ed‌ practices, and decades of clinical experience to provide hope and concrete guidance to anyone trapped in the revolving door of their own fears. Fear Traps provides breakthrough understandings and clear guidance for adolescents, adults, and seniors to systematically free themselves from what can feel like inescapable anxieties and fears."

—Richard Reckman, PhD
Past President, Ohio Psychological Association

"Dr. Stella is a master of self-esteem. She makes even our most closely held fears feel approachable and surmountable. When we feel small and paralyzed, she reminds us that we are the adult in the room, and we are capable of so much more than we think."

—Marian Rubin, LISW
Licensed Independent Social Worker

"A must-have resource for anyone stuck in a cycle of fear."

—Celia Oliver, PhD, PsyD
President of the New Hampshire Psychological Association

"In her book, Fear Traps, Dr. Stella captures the very foundation of common fears. Beyond that, she lays out a fantastic, detailed framework to attack it. This is an excellent resource for any therapist or patient wanting to improve their sense of self-esteem and self-efficacy."

—Ryan Schmidtz, MD
Schmidtz Psychiatry LLC

"Dr. Stella's book is one of hope. It chronicles the lives of several of her clients as they use the Courageous Brain Process to identify, navigate, and overcome the patterns that are stifling them. I've used Doctor Stella's process to remake my own emotional matrix. I can personally attest to its transformational power. I experience greater resilience, wellbeing, and deep swells of spontaneous happiness as a direct result of the practice. It's been a lifesaver for me."

—David Forrester
Creator of the Matrix, The Art of Emotional Healing

"Dr. Stella takes away the stigma often associated with trauma responses. She focuses on strengthening individuals—reminding them that they do have the power and inner resources to create positive changes in their lives and relationships. This book takes approaches I already use and combines them in a powerful way that someone can use on their own or to more easily participate in their therapy process."

—Dianne Latimer, PsyD
Licensed Psychologist

"Dr. Stella's Courageous Brain Process makes complex ideas so easy to understand. Her method has given me a sense of courage to face life's inevitable challenges without being constantly triggered by hurts of the past. I have used her strategies to free myself from perfectionism and fear of rejection that kept me living small. Now I am able to pursue my new opportunities and share myself freely."

—Carolyn Walters
Teacher of the Matrix, The Art of Emotional Healing

"You really can change the way your brain processes fear. Fear Traps shows you how."

—Lynda McConn, LPCC
Licensed Professional Clinical Counselor

"Dr. Stella read my mind so many times in these pages, but she never made me feel ashamed of my struggles. She has this unflappable, nothing-surprises-me type of attitude that calls others to live out what they're capable of. To those feeling constantly anxious, take a deep breath and start reading this book. This book is for you. It's precisely effective at calming us down because it's indelibly rooted in both brain research and real life. Dr. Stella shows us how to actually change the physical structures of our anxious brain, but she delivers this scientific discovery in a way that helps us feel lighter already."

—Carmen Berry, MSW
New York Times Bestselling Author /
When Helping You Is Hurting Me

"This book is an important contribution to self-help literature for those paralyzed by fear and anxiety. Dr. Stella's compelling personal examples and illustrious case material pull readers in as she guides them in how to form new neuropathways away from the brain's fear center—the essence of her Courageous Brain Process. With meditations that are not only behavioral and cognitive but also experiential and relational, her framework helps readers create lasting change. Therapists from a variety of orientations will find this a useful adjunct for their clients."

—Carol Lehman, PhD
Clinical Psychologist and Psychoanalyst

"Easy yet life-transforming for everyday situations."

—Lucy Allen, MSW, LISW
Former Chief Clinical Officer PsychBC

"Fear Traps is exactly what I've been looking for. Dr. Stella offers a concise way of understanding our brains with updated neuroscience research as backup. The concrete steps, easily tailored, will give my clients a plan that will offer them hope in relieving the often-debilitating effects of anxiety on their lives. This book will definitely guide my treatment of clients with anxiety and fear."

—Kathleen Grant, PsyD
Clinical Psychologist, Past President Cincinnati
Academy of Professional Psychology

FEAR TRAPS

ESCAPE THE TRIGGERS THAT KEEP YOU STUCK

NANCY STELLA
PhD, PsyD

Published by Berry Powell Press
Glendora, California
www.berrypowellpress.com

ISBN: 978-1-7363953-0-1 (paperback)
ISBN: 978-1-7363953-1-8 (ebook)
LCCN: 2021900036

The case studies in this book are composites from Dr. Stella's practice. All names and circumstances have been fictionalized to protect privacy.

Dedicated to Brooklyn, who embodies compassion.

CONTENTS

INTRODUCTION

How to Create a Courageous Brain

No one likes to feel afraid, but the truth is that fear itself isn't really the problem. The jolt of adrenaline that shocks us into immediate action when we feel afraid can save our lives. We run away (flee), defend ourselves with aggression (fight), or hold very still so that our opponent will lose interest in attacking us (freeze). Once the danger has passed and we've survived, our bodies automatically relax and resume a calm, confident state.

While the purpose of fear is to save our lives, chronic fear can severely damage us. Falling into a trap of fear day after day can shrink us into small shadows of who we were meant to be. Have you ever felt that way? You're not the only one.

When clients first come to me, they often express that they feel helpless against the familiar mistakes and painful patterns prevalent in their lives. Once trapped, we go round and round in a cycle of anxiety. Our self-defeating patterns of overreaction can literally ruin our relationships, careers, and health. I've seen chronic fear steal the joy and health from the hundreds of clients I've worked with over several decades. Some clients had already done years of therapy; others had tried multiple programs that never resolved their struggle. Up until recently, it wasn't clear why traditional methods didn't work for everyone.

Then there came a point where I, as a therapist, fell into my own fear trap. I got stuck for *years*. It baffled me! After all, I was supposed to be the one with the answers. I thought I understood how the brain worked and how to move on from trauma. Instead, the lowest point of my adult life showed me I was missing something important. For my clients and for myself, I set out to find it.

For years, I studied the relationship between our self-defeating patterns and the activity in our brains. The research revealed something key: In the early days of therapy, therapists believed that gaining insight was the best way to bring about transformation. Practically, this meant therapists would ask people to tell and retell their most traumatic stories until they gained insight about them.

However, newer scientific brain research has explained why this method sometimes did more harm than good. Rather than helping people gain transformative insight, this method repeatedly triggered the fear center of their brains without strengthening the brain's courage or resilience. When people came in with deep-seated fears and trauma, it wasn't uncommon for them to leave retraumatized rather than positively transformed.

The good news is that the latest discoveries on the human brain correct the miscalculations of this type of therapy. Better yet, the science proves that, with intentionality and consistency, you *can* change your brain and become unstuck. You and I can intentionally create courageous brains, no longer programmed to perpetually cycle in fear.

This was fantastic news! However, I knew the discovery alone wasn't enough. My clients were struggling deeply, and I knew how overwhelming those low points could feel. I realized they needed simple, approachable steps.

In response, I created the Courageous Brain Process (CBP)—a six-step method for overcoming old triggers and developing new courage. These six steps walk us through the process of *actually* carving new neuropathways into our brains. That means we can sidestep old pathways created by past traumatic experiences. No more being stuck!

This process has helped me move through multiple seasons of my own life, of which I wasn't sure I would ever escape. I've also shared this process with countless clients, who have experienced truly life-altering results. If you feel trapped in repetitious fears and inescapable failure, I want to assure you that the CBP can set you free. Your repetitive actions and mental focus will change your life by changing the way your brain processes fear.

To get the most out of this book, I recommend you read it through, as each chapter builds on the previous one. If you have trouble with a specific fear, I'd also recommend that you pay extra attention to the issues described in that targeted chapter.

While there are many fears that can beset us, I've selected the six most common I've seen in my clients: fear of being alone, fear of being rejected, fear of confrontation, fear of being ignored, fear of failure, and fear of the unknown. The method used for addressing these can easily be adapted to any other fear you may encounter.

You have the opportunity to reenvision your life. With the CBP, you will be empowered to make different choices and build new paths to success in your relationships, goals, and personal life.

After using the process outlined in this book, you will have the power to:

- Identify the root cause of your current fear(s)
- Identify why and how you are triggered
- Objectively evaluate your emotions rather than being controlled by them
- Break free from old, self-defeating behaviors
- Learn tools to help you respond in a healthy way
- Design the life you want to live, equipped to face new challenges

Join me in a journey that takes you to a place of strength and freedom, no longer trapped by chronic fear.

The Purpose of Healthy Fear

The purpose of healthy fear is to get us out of danger as quickly as possible. When our sympathetic nervous system is triggered by a sense of danger, our breath becomes rapid and shallow. Our heart rate increases, and blood flows away from our organs and out to our arms and legs, so we can respond quickly. Once the threat has been resolved, our bodies are meant to return to a state of calm or a sense of well-being. When we are in a relaxed state, our parasympathetic nervous system is activated. Our heart rate slows, blood moves away from our muscles to our organs, and we breathe more deeply. We return to a state of calm that promotes critical thinking, empathy, health, and happiness.

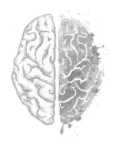

Are You Afraid of Being Alone?

*Once we recognize what it is we are feeling, once we recognize
we can feel deeply, love deeply, can feel joy, then we will
demand that all parts of our lives produce that kind of joy.*
—Audre Lorde

It was a typical Friday afternoon—my day off from my work as a therapist. I was working in my garden, enjoying time for myself. The sun was bright, and I wore a large-brimmed straw hat to shade my face. I dug up the front flower bed to plant irises.

When I was nearly finished, I heard a ring from my landline. Hurrying inside, I recognized the voice of my sister-in-law, Anna. "Nancy, did you and Gary order new furniture?" I could easily picture the wrinkle between her deep-green eyes that always showed up when she was perplexed.

"No, we didn't. Why?"

"Well, a furniture store in town called me asking if I'd ordered some items. They lost the info on the actual customer, but since my brother and I have the same last name, they somehow got in touch with me."

I was stumped. "Who did they say the customer was?"

"Some guy named Barry."

"Well, we didn't order anything from that store." I pushed my hair out of my eyes.

"Would you mind calling them just to make sure?" she asked.

I agreed and dialed their number. I let them know the order wasn't from us, and I went back to planting my irises.

I had met Gary when I entered graduate school. He was a handsome, older professor, and I immediately felt safe and accepted. It was easy to trust his affection and devotion. We married four years later, and then we adopted two baby girls—one from Honduras and the other from Guatemala. It was a joyous time in my life, becoming a happy family. Or so I thought.

As I dug into the ground, I realized that "Barry" could be mistaken for Gary, which was my husband's name. Why would he buy furniture and not tell me? And then it hit me with clarity brighter than the sun above me. If Gary bought furniture, it would be for living somewhere other than with our two daughters and me. I tried to stop my mind from quickly putting the pieces together, but everything so easily fell into place. My husband of twenty years was having an affair.

Gary was often out late ("The meeting ran long"). His closet was almost empty of clothes ("I keep them in the trunk of the car so it's easier to go to the gym"). When he traveled to Europe on business, he could not be reached ("The apartment where I stay doesn't have a phone"). The list had been growing, but I had kept my eyes and heart tightly shut. On this day, however, out in the garden, I could hide from it no longer: Gary must have another place in town—a love nest that he was furnishing for his mistress.

Sinking down onto the dirt, I wept uncontrollably. I could no longer deny Gary's betrayal. It was the final tug on my loose emotional thread, and there in the garden, I came undone. He'd broken my trust. He had another lover. The life I'd built with him was a sham.

And there was something else—even more terrifying. I felt the bottom drop out of my soul. Darkness filled my body. A jolt of terror sped through me. How could I survive without him?

I lost track of time. I don't know how long I cried in our back-yard. Fortunately, I was able to pull myself together before my teenage daughters got home from school. I greeted them as usual, as if nothing had changed. We went about our afternoon like it was any other day in our lives. I gave them a snack, as always, and the girls went to their rooms to do their homework and listen to music.

While they were occupied, I went into our bedroom with the intention of making it my bedroom. Quietly, I brought down a suitcase. Opening the drawers on his side of the bureau, I was stunned to see how few items remained. Several drawers were completely empty. My sadness gave way to anger—at myself. What kind of woman doesn't notice her husband has moved out?

I went to his side of the closet. The only clothes still hanging there were a couple of shirts he never wore anymore, a heavy winter coat that was of no use to him at that moment, and some old hiking boots. I grabbed them and shoved them into the suitcase, with plenty of room to spare. In the bathroom, I snatched up the few remnants left there, and quickly closed the suitcase. A whoosh of his cologne washed over my face—a scent I had come to know so well. And yet, the man had become a stranger. I was furious with myself for letting him play me as a fool.

As the sun began to set, the anger I felt toward myself became smoldering rage toward Gary. I placed the suitcase behind the recliner in anticipation of his arrival just before dinner. I was like a cat about to pounce on an unsuspecting mouse. My ears were attuned to the sounds of Gary's car pulling into the driveway. As expected, I heard his car first and then the sound of the car door closing. Before Gary could get to the front door, I picked up the suitcase and met him just outside.

He smiled at me like he always did when he came home. Then, looking down, he saw the suitcase.

"All of your things are in here," I said and shoved it toward him. "Go stay at your *other* place."

He looked stunned at first, his mouth open like a fish out of water. A second later, resignation spread across his face upon realizing that I had finally figured it all out.

"As far as I'm concerned, the marriage is over," I said with disdain. Cold and calm, I appeared to be completely in control.

For a man who was ordinarily very articulate, he could find no words to say. He didn't ask to talk to his daughters. In fact, he said nothing at all. He simply picked up the suitcase, turned around, and walked back to his car in submission.

I called the girls into the living room, and they came in with confused looks on their faces. "Wasn't that Dad?" the oldest asked. I nodded and motioned them to sit down.

I explained what their father had done. Assuring them that he would always be their father, I added, "But I will no longer be his wife."

The girls didn't look as surprised as I expected. They were more willing to see what had been happening than I had been. I pretended I was glad to see him go, but behind the veneer, I didn't feel like an adult who could adequately care for her children. As if taken back in time, I was reliving the trauma of my childhood, alone and abandoned by my parents. My daughters looked to me for guidance, while I wished some other grownup would walk into the room and take care of all three of us. I assured them with a calm voice, but deep inside I was terrified that I might come completely undone.

Falling Into the Fear Trap

After my marriage ended, I got stuck in a fear trap for a long time—nearly five years. They were five very difficult years for me. I spiraled and became anxious, questioning my competence and identity. Even though I was an adult, I felt like a little girl again, lost and overlooked in a confusing world. Because I didn't yet understand that my brain was re-experiencing some deep ruts of childhood abandonment, I believed all my past fears were telling me the truth about the present. I lost faith in myself and my ability to handle challenges.

My mind filled with troubling questions. Can I survive this? Will I be able to I support myself and my daughters as a single mother? Will we have to move? Was I capable of helping my daughters through this terrible time?

I felt like I was falling apart. I imagined lying in bed forever, unable to cope, unable to deal with the devastating sense of betrayal. Why didn't I see this coming? Why was I so blind to his lies? I felt humiliated. How could I face the world?

Now I can look back and clearly understand that I had fallen into a fear trap. Specifically, I fell into a fear trap of abandonment. And although I was a successful therapist at the time, I didn't yet have the tools to help myself. I had a lot to learn before I was able to resolve my deep anxiety and build a new and better life for myself and my daughters. And what I learned—what helped me escape my fear trap—is what I'm going to teach you in this book. I'll give you a spoiler: it all comes down to your brain.

What's Going On in Our Brains?

The autonomic nervous system is responsible for our flight, fight, and freeze responses. As the name implies, it is automatic in responding. There are two major parts to this system. The parasympathetic system kicks in when we are relaxed and rested. Blood moves away from our muscles and to our organs. The sympathetic nervous system is activated when we are energized. Blood moves to our muscles, increases our heart rate, and triggers activating hormones, preparing us for potentially dangerous or stressful situations. The vagus nerve is a cranial nerve that interfaces with the parasympathetic nervous system and also contributes to our relaxation response.

It's critical to understand the basics of how the brain processes fear. Throughout this book, we will focus on two parts of the brain: the amygdala and the frontal lobe.

The amygdala is rather small for the powerful role it plays in our lives. It is almond shaped, comprised of two amygdalae, one situated in each brain hemisphere in the temporal lobes. It holds the brain's fear and stress responses, and influences how our memories are stored. It's small but mighty. It takes over when we believe our physical or psychological survival is being threatened.

The frontal lobe, aptly named, is at the front of our brains and is the home of our ability to reason, problem solve, relate to others, and negotiate our actions and reactions. When we are babies, our frontal lobes aren't fully developed yet. As we grow bigger, so do our cognitive and reasoning abilities. Once we reach adulthood, we should have full access to the power of our frontal lobes.

I commonly refer to the amygdala as our fear center. If you've ever jumped out of the way of a speeding car or ran screaming for help from a would-be attacker, you have your amygdala to thank. You didn't have time to think as if you were in a dance lesson: *Oh, I should move this foot here and that foot there.* With no time to plan, your amygdala took over and got you out of harm's way.

When we are in danger, our brains automatically empower the amygdala to protect us and cut off connection with the frontal lobe. This is important because we need to react to danger instantaneously, not take time to be overly thoughtful. After the life-threatening danger has passed, we are supposed to calm down and regain our ability to reason, problem solve, and process what happened to us.

Memories, especially traumatic ones, are recorded in our brains through neuropathways. Imagine neuropathways as paths running through a meadow. The first time you walk over the grass, there may not be much of a trace left behind you. But if you walk this same route repeatedly, a path will form as the grass recedes. The same is true of our brain as it records our thoughts and experiences.

Now imagine that a large, heavy truck speeds over the same path. The tires cut deep into the earth and leave a well-defined trail. Painful memories are like massive trucks digging deeply into your brain, leaving lifelong neuropathways behind. As long as your brain is stuck in these neuropathways, you will most likely repeat the self-defeating patterns of a fear trap over and over again.

To make matters worse, many of us have had traumatic experiences during which we didn't get the support we needed. It's not necessarily true that our parents or caregivers didn't *want* to help us. When we were little, we may not have known how to communicate our needs so the adults around us understood how to help us.

It's also possible that the adults in our lives never learned how to ask for help or calm *themselves* down during times of crisis. Therefore, they were unable to teach us. Regardless of the reason, we can grow up without knowing how to effectively cope when our amygdala takes over and how to soothe ourselves so the more reasonable parts of our brains kick back in.

One of the most significant discoveries I found was that something in the present—anything scary or even something totally mundane—can remind us of a past event in which we were harmed or in danger of harm. This association is called a trigger.

When you are triggered, the amygdala reacts as if your life is in danger *now*—even though you're not—because you were in danger in the past. Trapped in deep ruts of trauma in the amygdala, we lose access to the frontal lobe and our ability to realistically assess the situation and effectively respond. Instead, we misjudge and overreact—often repeatedly.

Living out of the traumatic past as if it's in the present can severely damage our relationships and hinder our goals, but we can't seem to calm down and respond any other way. This scenario is what I call a fear trap. If you don't know how to effectively deal with fear, you could have the same experience I did—being physically and emotionally trapped in a state of fear for years.

> *Something in the present— anything scary or even something totally mundane— can remind us of a past event in which we were harmed or in danger of harm. This association is called a trigger.*

The Courageous Brain Process

Something good came out of my personal struggle. It led me to the missing piece myself and my clients needed to experience true breakthrough in our lives.

Therapists used to ask their clients to talk through their most traumatic stories, over and over. The idea was that if they reflected on their past, they'd gain *insight*: a realization of something new and redemptive they couldn't see before. Therapists believed insight alone would heal their clients' trauma. And they weren't *entirely* wrong—gaining insight on past experiences *has* helped many people move towards healing. But our latest brain science explains why this often did more harm than good or left the healing process incomplete. This method unwittingly encouraged clients to walk those deep pathways of trauma repeatedly. Rather than healing, this method made those neuropathways even deeper, constantly bringing people back to their fear center.

Old neuropathways tell us, "When you're triggered, you respond this way," over and over again—even if that response is self-destructive. New neuropathways say, "When you're triggered, you don't have to respond the same way you always have. Let's look at the situation and decide what response will help you and others."

The Courageous Brain Process (CBP) teaches people how to practically create these new neuropathways in their everyday lives. It has completely transformed the way I face life's inevitable challenges.

These are the simple steps that help us calm down more quickly, think critically in moments of stress, and break old cycles:

- Step One: Tell Your Story
- Step Two: Identify Your Triggers
- Step Three: Describe Patterns of Self-Sabotage
- Step Four: Imagine the Worst-Case Scenario
- Step Five: Create a Courageous Brain
- Step Six: Live Free of the Fear Trap

How do these six steps create new neuropathways that free us? Research has revealed that the brain *physically changes* when we repeat self-directed thoughts and exercises. My program gives you exercises that create those physical changes and redirect where your thoughts go in stress.

Imagine these new grooves as off-ramps from the major highway you have been forced to follow all this time. You'll finally be able to drive off or even around the deep grooves that were made years ago. This process has freed me and so many others from their fear traps.

At first, these six steps may seem deceptively simple, and you might wonder whether they can work in your life as well as I claim. Don't let the simplicity fool you—the CBP works. You will learn how to break self-defeating cycles and create the new patterns you desire. Rather than being at the mercy of your kneejerk reactions, you'll be empowered to recognize triggers, break free from old patterns, and move beyond the places where you've been stuck.

Neuroplasticity is a Game Changer

We would be doomed to walk the same old paths if not for one game-changing discovery: we can actually change the structure and function of our brains. Scientists and therapists previously thought those pathways—or neural networks—were set in stone once we reached adulthood, but they aren't. Ever since the discovery of neuroplasticity—the ability of pathways in the brain to change—we have known that the brain can form new connections and patterns and even unlearn old ones.

You can change your brain and your life, but success requires action on your part. It is vitally important for you to do the exercises in each chapter, not just once but over and over and over. Just like making a new trail through the field of grass, repetition is the key. New pathways will be created over time, and you'll have a brand-new ability to confront and manage the fears that have kept you trapped. I invite you to take this journey into a truly effective, simple process that actually changes the way your brain processes fear. You will be empowered to a higher level of confidence and competence than you've enjoyed before. I will use my own experience to show you how I conquered my fear of being alone.

Step One: Tell Your Story

The first step in the CBP is finding a safe place to tell your story. When you tell your story, you have the opportunity to identify the triggers that keep you stuck. You may tell your story in a private way such as through journaling, art, music, or another format. But for the deepest healing to occur, it's critical to eventually tell someone else your story. This could be a therapist, spiritual adviser, trusted friend, or family member. We need to feel accepted and believed when we share what has happened to us. There is healing in the telling—in having someone pay attention and listen to us speak.

I always ask my clients to tell me the story of their past. Understanding our past increases our awareness of present patterns. When you tell your story, do not get hung up on trying to get it "just right." Trust your gut when you tell your story. It's your story. Claim it.

When I was a child, my parents, my younger sister, and I lived with my father's mother. As an Italian-speaking immigrant, she didn't know how to navigate the English-speaking world and never felt at home in the United States. When I was five, my father passed away suddenly. Soon after, my mother slid into a life of despair, addiction, and alcoholism. I had a one-and-a-half-year-old sister for whom I felt responsible. I always felt loved by my grandmother, and I know she tried to protect me and my sister. Yet she couldn't prevent us from feeling the emotional pain of losing our father. Nor could she shelter us from experiencing repetitive abandonment by our mother, who was in and out of psych wards due to her own inner pain and addictions.

Fearing something would happen to my grandmother as well, I cried every day from the moment I left for school until the moment I returned home. I didn't know what would happen to my sister and me if my grandmother died. I was too young to take care of my sister or myself. While most children are afraid on occasion, I lived in constant fear of abandonment. We call this a core emotional wound: a form of trauma early in life that affects us into adulthood.

Step Two: Identify Your Triggers

A core emotional wound is captured in our brains. It impacts not only our memories but the actual ways in which our brain is structured. Traumatic memories are recorded in the amygdala. When we are triggered, our brains mistakenly tell us that we are in the same level of danger as we were in the past.

We're suddenly transported back in time to relive the trauma of our past. We may or may not even remember the actual event, but we are overwhelmed by the emotion we felt during the awful experience. We overreact and respond out of proportion to the present threat. If the painful memory is repeatedly triggered, our amygdala literally grows in size and influence. We can get stuck, seeing no way out.

My First Trigger: The Scent of Gary's Cologne

I had every right to be upset and hurt by my husband's actions. But now I associated his betrayal with the scent of his cologne that was so pronounced while I packed up his clothes. This scent didn't simply remind me of what he did, but it flung me back into my childhood despair. It brought me back in time to the age I was when I first experienced the trauma of abandonment and loneliness.

Rather than feeling like an adult woman negotiating the terms of her divorce, I sat next to my attorney feeling as if I were a little girl. For that moment, I was no longer able to reason at my true chronological age. I reasoned and reacted as if I were a child.

We can be triggered by smells, sounds, touches, and tastes. We might see a color, a piece of clothing, or another visual reminder of an old trauma. Like a trapdoor, that reminder pulls us back in time to the age when we were first wounded.

If you were three when something difficult happened to you, you will reason and emotionally react like a three year old—not the adult you are today. If you were thirteen, you'll reason with a teenage brain and respond with adolescent emotions. If you were twenty-two when you had an accident or suffered abuse, you'll be thrown back to your early twenties without the wisdom and maturity you have accrued throughout your life. Your reactions can surprise you—and those around you.

My Second Trigger: Gary's Voice on the Phone

I became triggered by the sound of his voice when Gary and I talked on the phone. In my ear was the voice of the man I had trusted completely. I planned to raise our girls and grow old together. But now, the sound plunged me into the despair of reliving his

> *I realized I was overreacting, but I couldn't stop my reaction.*

betrayal and the emotional loss of my parents. It got so bad at one point that I insisted my attorney speak on the phone for me. I was too overwhelmed to hear his voice. I realized I was overreacting, but I couldn't stop my reaction. I thought I was going crazy.

The good news is that in time, I realized I wasn't crazy. I was overreacting because of an emotional trigger. It's possible to recognize in the moment that we're experiencing particular emotions because we're being triggered and our brain is stuck in a pattern of fear. You can create a new pattern that is not based on the fears of a child but on the confidence you have in yourself as an adult.

Step Three: Describe Patterns of Self-Sabotage

Because our brains aren't fully developed until adulthood, the coping methods we develop as children are rarely helpful when we grow into adults. These need to be revised as we grow older and gain more insight from self-reflection.

The flaws in our outdated coping mechanisms are intensified when we are triggered. We develop behavioral patterns that sabotage our adult happiness and success. Living in jeopardy of being triggered by a reoccurring pattern is not a quality way to spend our days, nor does it help us establish stable relationships. We lose confidence in our capacity to deal with life as adults. Does it seem like no matter how hard you've tried, you're back in that same painful place again?

- You thought this relationship would be different, but it turns out to be the same old story with the same sad ending.
- You thought you'd finally found your dream job, but before long, you realized you'll never be recognized for your efforts.
- You thought you'd gotten through to your teenager, but then this morning, the two of you had another huge fight.
- You thought you had forgiven your spouse for the harsh words spoken, but you are still fuming inside.
- You thought if you tried hard enough, you could lose weight on a new program, but once again, you gained back all of the pounds you lost and then some.

Often you can experience success in some areas of your life while being triggered in other areas. You may have a brilliant career but find yourself continually disappointed in your intimate relationships. Or you may have a satisfying marriage but be in constant conflict with your boss or coworkers. How is it that you can succeed in some areas of your life but still can't overcome that one problem that keeps bringing you to a place of defeat? You're stuck in a pattern you can't seem to resolve.

Self-Sabotage Pattern One: Defeating Self-Talk

It's certainly appropriate to be upset when crises occur in our lives: the death of a loved one, the loss of a job, a needed surgery, another event we cannot avoid. Finding safe spaces to process our grief is critical to the healing process. During times of stress, many turn to individual or group therapy for support. Once the crisis has been properly dealt with, we achieve a new equilibrium and no longer experience fear and dread.

But I didn't calm down for years. I was caught in a pattern of self-doubt and the fear trap of abandonment. Through the divorce and for several years after, I could not get my footing. This extended suffering was not just the reality of divorce and starting over, but it went on because I mismanaged my own feelings. I was a competent adult when Gary left me; I had to regain my ability to function according to my actual age and not behave like a terrified little girl.

As is often the case, my head filled with negative self-talk. I'd tell myself:

- I can't live without him.
- How can I make decisions without him?
- Everyone must be laughing at me for taking so long to see through his lies.
- What is wrong with me?
- I'll never be happy again.

The more I listened to myself, the more upset I became. Deeper into a fear trap I fell, as I literally dug the fear-based neuropathways deeper into my brain. The more I repeated those statements to myself, the more frightened I became.

Self-Sabotage Pattern Two: Blaming My Husband for All of My Problems

In addition to being afraid, I also become consumed with rage and the desire to punish my ex. I blamed Gary for ruining our family and my life, and I wanted to see him suffer. More negative self-talk developed, only this version was all about him. Round and round I went in my mind, reviewing every wrong he had done to me yet never able to resolve my feelings. As a result, I unwittingly increased the extent of my pain, and I lengthened the time I suffered. I focused on what I lost. I could have recovered faster and more easily if I had known the steps I use today.

I eventually saw that my anger was also part of my fear trap. If we feel helpless to protect ourselves, we can turn fear into anger. This can make us feel that we're protecting ourselves, but we're not.

We simply hurt ourselves by flooding our systems with stress hormones, which make us feel miserable, keep us from resolving our problems, and damage our immune systems. When we live under the control of the amygdala, we can only fight, flee, or freeze—primitive reactions that do not lead to strong relationships or patterns for success in other areas of our lives.

Looking back, I'm not proud of the way I behaved. I realized I had to do something about my fear and anger or I'd become a bitter woman, helpless to run her own life. I acknowledged I had a problem that needed to be addressed.

If you find yourself consumed by circular feelings such as fear, anger, sadness, and self-criticism, it's time to see that you're stuck in a pattern of self-hurting. Negative memories deeply etched into your brain are being triggered. None of us can solve a problem that we pretend doesn't exist. Is it time to acknowledge that you are stuck in an emotional conundrum that warrants your attention? You need help and deserve help. It's not possible to meaningfully move forward while stuck in a fear trap.

Step Four: Imagine the Worst-Case Scenario

When trapped in fear, we subconsciously assume that—be it physically or psychologically—we will not survive this. Death, of course, can be a terrifying prospect and will eventually occur for all of us. But it's important to accept the fact that death is the only thing that isn't survivable. Everything else can be overcome.

I used to live as if I was in danger when my life was not actually threatened. My clients often feel the same. I've been told by clients that they could not survive if their spouse left them or if they lost their job. They live captive to imagined outcomes they believe will destroy them physically and psychologically.

But you are no longer a child, dependent on your parents. Sure, being abandoned as a child was a serious threat to your survival. But now? You have the ability to take care of yourself in ways you couldn't as a child. I, for example, was able to say to myself, *Nancy, you are no longer a child. Despite what Gary did, you have more power and capacity for self-care and protection than you did when you were small. You might feel as if you can't survive feeling abandoned, but, in fact, you can.*

Once I realized this, my paralyzing fear started to recede, and my frontal lobe kicked back in. I was no longer at the mercy of my terrorized amygdala and could search for more sophisticated solutions to my self-defeating patterns.

It is horrible to be betrayed by someone you love and trust. Believe me, I know. But while it was excruciatingly painful for a period of time, it did not destroy me. In fact, in the process of facing the truth and going through the divorce, I became stronger. I am braver and more willing to see things as they truly are rather than hide in denial. My life today is much happier than it was when I was in a marriage with someone who was purposefully deceiving me. Once I realized I could survive, I did—I survived quite well.

I find the same is true of my clients. Once they recognize they are immensely braver, stronger, and more competent than they currently believe, a new sense of resilience fills them. The fears that kept them trapped lose their grip, and life becomes a series of options rather than immediate threats.

Once you imagine the worst that could realistically happen and realize you are capable of dealing with the outcome, you will find a new freedom and confidence you've not known before.

A Word of Caution

I encourage those who have had significant and repeated trauma to do this program with a licensed mental health professional. Being triggered is upsetting and frightening. If you've been physically or sexually abused as a child, you may benefit from therapy, spiritual direction, or support-group assistance.

Step Five: Create a Courageous Brain

When we focus on our self-confidence and possibilities, rather on our fears, our brain builds new neuropathways that reinforce that confidence. In turn, those new, positive neuropathways cause our thoughts to become more positive. For many years, the vague idea of thinking positively has been touted as a way to create a better future for oneself. But the hazy ideal of thinking positive thoughts isn't enough to make a long-term change. Research studies have demonstrated that changing our brains requires a *certain type of mental focus and visualization.*

We are able to focus our thoughts and transfer energy from our fear center to other parts of our brain that increase a sense of safety, decision-making options, and spiritual enlightenment. Each time we do so, new neuropathways that lead the activity away from the amygdala are added and expanded. The amygdala can actually shrink. Meanwhile, other parts of our brains associated with logic, emotional regulation, problem-solving, and feelings of peace can physically increase in size.

As with learning any new skill, practice makes perfect. In the same way you learn how to drive a car, cook a new dish, or play the piano, you can learn new ways of coping, reacting, and feeling. *Repetition is the key.*

In each chapter, I provide an exercise specific to a different common fear. The exercises in this book are called "focused meditation"; they use the power of our focused attention to change how our brain processes each fear. Here's a heads-up, though: the initial hope you feel doing the exercises will likely wane. It's easy to lose faith in the process if we don't experience immediate results. Learning a new skill takes practice and effort.

The good news is that each time we complete a meditation, our wounds heal a little bit more. Our lives are transformed as our brains are restructured. With repetition and commitment, we can change the way our emotional neuronal network is wired. This is why my approach succeeds where other programs have failed in bringing about lasting change. Taking repetitive, small steps, these practical exercises teach us how to break free from fear traps and change our way of perceiving and behaving.

Focused Meditation Exercise:

The following is a fifteen-minute exercise. I recommend you read over this exercise first and then set a timer to remind yourself to go to the next section. It may take once or twice to get the hang of it, but by working through this meditation on a daily basis, you'll have the power to change your brain and create new pathways. When triggered, you'll be able to recover more quickly. With repetition, you may be able to sidestep the trigger altogether.

Escape the Fear Trap of Being Alone
Begin

Start by getting into a comfortable position. Breathe in through your nose and exhale through your mouth. You may be breathing shallowly, primarily from your chest.

Focus attention on breathing deeply into your abdomen. It may take a while to relax to the point where your stomach expands and retracts with each slow breath. Continue to breathe in through your nose and out through your mouth.

5-Minute Mark

Now that you are more relaxed, think of one person in your life, past or present, who you consider a safe person. It could be a best friend. It could be a child, a spouse, a teacher, or a mentor.

Think of this person as you breathe in and out. After a few more breaths, I want you to imagine an invisible string that connects from your heart to theirs. Experience the connection and the warmth of their presence and acceptance. Let their love permeate your body and mind (concept from *The Invisible String* by Patricia Karst, published by Little, Brown Books for Young Readers in 2000).

7-Minute Mark

Select a second person who is or has been safe for you. Keep the thread connected to the first person and attach another string to the second person. Think of this person and how you feel accepted and loved by him/her. Again, it can be anyone—someone you work with, a relative, or a childhood friend.

Think of both of these people as you breathe in and breathe out. Let yourself soak up the love traveling through the strings that connect you with these two safe and loving people. Remember that when you are frightened, it's easy to feel you are alone, even though there are people in your life who accept you and love you.

9-Minute Mark

Add a third person to your meditation. Think of another person who nurtures you or has nurtured you in the past. Choose someone who fills you with a sense of encouragement and hope.

It can be someone who inspires you to be all you can be, someone who believes in you even when things are difficult. This is a person to whom you can go when you feel lonely and afraid. Connect a string to them and know they are in your life now or in your memories, forever available to you. Sit within the warmth of these three people.

11-Minute Mark

Maintain the connection between you and these three safe and loving people. Imagine yourself as a fourth person who accepts and loves you. Add yourself to the circle so that you now have four people connected to you by strings. Give yourself the love and acceptance you need and deserve.

- On the inhale, say, "I accept myself completely."
- On the exhale, say, "I am strong and capable."
- Repeat this affirmation:
- I accept myself completely.

- I am strong and capable.

14-Minute Mark

Even though it may feel like a small step, you have been changed through this meditation. Your brain has been soothed. The fear center of your brain has been diverted, and your frontal lobe has been stimulated. A new, albeit small, neuropathway has been formed. You will strengthen this pathway every time you do this meditation.

Now wiggle your fingers and toes and slowly bring yourself back to the outside world. Take a few more deep breaths. You are now ready to engage with your life, newly energized to face whatever comes your way.

Meditation Completed

I recommend you do this meditation every day for forty days, as it will strengthen the neuropathway and create a new habit in your brain. When you feel alone, it will be easier to soothe yourself and remind yourself that you have people in your life who love you. Most importantly, you'll more easily recall that you love yourself and believe in your own strength and resilience.

Step Six: Live Free of the Fear Trap

Imagine a life where you could respond to any circumstance with a calm brain that makes healthy decisions. That's what I want for my life, and I suspect you do too. I had been so afraid of being alone that I closed my eyes to what was really happening in my marriage. My goal, however, is to live in truth—even when it is difficult or challenging—because I know I can handle what comes my way.

With this new perspective, I was able to create a fulfilling new life for myself and my daughters. It took a while to realize I no longer had to be at the mercy of triggers. I no longer had to relive horrible experiences from the past. The truth is, rarely does our worst fear occur. And yet the anticipation can draw us into a fear trap. When we realize that we can indeed survive, suddenly we are released from the self-limiting fears we foster in our minds.

Five years after that awful day in my garden, I received a letter from Gary. As I held it up, a gentle whiff of his cologne reached my nose. This time, it had no effect on me. I wasn't triggered at all.

The letter told me he had remarried, and while it stung a bit, I was very happy with my life as it was. I had started to date by that time, and I was enjoying new relationships. But I knew I no longer needed a man in order to survive. Holding the letter, I walked through my garden. The irises I'd planted were in full bloom—beautiful, resilient, and lifting their flowers to the sun. I smiled with a contentment and sense of self-confidence I never thought possible until I broke free of my fear trap. You can do the same.

Key Points

- As children, we needed adults to nurture and protect us.
- We also needed adult role models to show us how to deal with frightening and difficult situations.
- Without proper role models, we can grow into adulthood without knowing how to properly cope with our fears.
- Memories of past trauma, including the painful emotions we experienced, are recorded in our brains through neuropathways.
- These traumatic memories and emotions are called core emotional wounds. We can carry these into adulthood.
- A trigger occurs when an event in the present reminds us of a past trauma.
- When triggered, our amygdala (fear center) can take over control of our brain.
- When the amygdala is in control, we lose contact with our frontal lobe, which has the ability to reason, observe, negotiate, and problem solve. This is what I call the fear trap.
- When caught in a fear trap, we relive our past trauma. We can think and behave at the age we were when the trauma occurred.
- We know we've been triggered when we overreact to a present event or situation.
- Negative self-talk strengthens the neuropathways of trauma, and it deepens the self-defeating patterns in our behaviors and attitudes.
- Scientists used to believe the brain could not change, especially as we got older. They were wrong. We can add new neuropathways in our brain that reroute the energy flow away from our fear traps.

- We create these new pathways through repetitious mental focus and visualization.
- New neuropathways can provide us the opportunity to break free of self-defeating patterns and create new patterns that empower us.

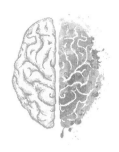

Are You Afraid of Rejection?

And the day came when the risk to remain tight in a bud
became more painful than the risk it took to blossom.
—Anais Nin

Isabella's voice over the phone was shrill with desperation. "Dr. Stella? I've heard you can help people who struggle with high anxiety. And I'm really upset. Can you see me today?"

Later that afternoon, Isabella was in my office, wringing her hands, and looking at me with red-rimmed eyes. At five-foot-nine with long, auburn hair and green eyes, she had the presence of a model, yet she seemed awkward in her own skin. As soon as she settled in, I asked her to share with me what had upset her.

Step One: Tell Your Story

Isabella did not hesitate to tell me she had recently met a man named Jack. A smile came over her face. "He is so wonderful. We've only been dating for about three months, but no one has gotten to me like Jack. He's perhaps the most articulate and level-headed man I've ever met. I feel so safe with him."

She shook her head. "Well, I *did* feel safe with him, until this week. Jack left on a business trip and told me he would call while he was away. The first night, he left me a message to say he was busy but wanted me to know he was thinking of me and would call the next day. The second day came and went with no call. Yesterday was the third day with no call, and I had a total meltdown last night. I was too embarrassed to let anyone at the divorce recovery group know I'm acting this way. But I called my friend Sarah, and she recommended I call you. I'm a mess."

I smiled. "I am glad you reached out. So it's been a few days without word from Jack?"

She nodded. "I'm so upset and anxious. Part of me knows I'm over-reacting. But I can't get a grip on my feelings. I feel desperate and needy."

I assured Isabella that together we could address this obstacle. Then I asked her to describe her fear. "I'm afraid he'll abandon me and…" she said, pausing. "I don't know if I can cope with losing him." She looked outside through the window.

"You're afraid you'll fall apart?"

She nodded. "What if I can't handle this? I barely got through my divorce. I just don't think I can take another traumatic disappointment. Plus, I just started a new job. I can't fall into a depression or let this affect my work. What if I lose my job because I can't deal with this?"

Isabella was terrified she wouldn't be able to survive the loss of this new relationship. Survival is the most powerful need we all have. Every one of us fears something could come into our lives that we wouldn't be able to survive—physically, financially, or psychologically.

I asked her about her childhood. Isabella had an older brother with whom she wasn't close. She described her father as quickly angered, easily brought to tears, and rarely happy for any length of time. Her mother, a rather cold woman of few words, was born and raised in Britain and re-turned there frequently to visit. On one such trip, her mother met a man.

"My mother returned demanding a divorce," Isabella explained. "I was thirteen at the time and begged her not to leave, but she said she was miserable in the marriage. When I asked my mom if I could go with her to London, she said no."

Isabella took a breath before continuing. "We were all standing in the living room as she left—each of us in our own pain. My father was in shock, my brother stood off to the side glaring, and I clung to her. She looked down at me and said, 'Someday, when you're in love, you'll understand.' And she was gone. I turned to my stricken father. 'Why don't you fight for her? Go stop her!' He got emotional and left the room.

"My seventeen-year-old brother looked at me and said, 'You're so stupid. That only happens in movies.' He went into his room and slammed the door.

"My mother's absence crippled all of us. My dad shut down and became very bitter. My brother quit high school, got a job at a hardware store, and moved out. He's still single, and my dad never remarried—both are very pessimistic about women in general. I call them every now and then," Isabella told me, "but nothing I do seems to make either of them happy, so it's rather futile. Is it any wonder that I never learned how to effectively handle emotional intensity or communication?"

Isabella left for college with the mission of finding a partner who was nothing like either of her parents, especially her father. "I wanted a man who wasn't controlled by his emotions. My father also gave up on my mother too early. I met Paul met during my sophomore year of college. It was easy being around him because his moods were so predictable. We married when I was twenty-two years old—six months after graduation." She thought she had found the perfect man in Paul. He was stoic and stable. Everything her father wasn't.

The Price of Loneliness

Being abandoned and being rejected are two different experiences. However, it's easy to see how both can leave us feeling alone. Feelings of loneliness, isolation, and disconnection are at epidemic proportions. Cigna conducted a study in 2018 asking twenty thousand adults to complete UCLA's loneliness scale. The results were shocking. Here are the findings:

- Almost half of the respondents reported feeling alone or left out sometimes or always.
- One in four stated they rarely or never feel that people understand them.
- Approximately forty-seven percent felt they did not have meaningful in-person interactions daily.
- Forty-three percent reported feelings of isolation from others.
- The loneliest groups were single parents and adults between the ages of eighteen and twenty-two.

The cause of our feelings of isolation is not always clear, but we do know loneliness is correlated with increased rates of depression, anxiety, addiction, suicide, and poor health.

Recognize that relationships are not instant; they take time to build. We live in an impatient culture—we want instant gratification. But it has been estimated that it takes about eight conversations with someone before a friendship is started. Relationships require time to develop trust, learn about one another, and connect.

Isolation is a problem because humans are social animals by nature. We have created a society that emphasizes our need for others. We seek out interactions; we seek to build family; we seek to build a cooperative society in which we care for others and others care for us. As a result, rejection and isolation are naturally painful.

Living behind walls—even in the relationships we already have—is a terrible price to pay for self-defense. Of course, we don't want to be hurt or feel the anxiety of not being accepted. Isolation and disconnection seem to protect us from that. However, since we are hardwired for connection, it is impossible for most of us to be truly satisfied when we feel disconnected. Is this a price you want to pay?

Step Two: Identify Your Triggers

I asked Isabella to continue her story. After the birth of their first child, Isabella realized the stability she had seen in Paul was actually emotional rigidity. In fact, he had little tolerance for emotional expression of any kind; he viewed it as a sign of weakness. Paul criticized Isabella when she became frustrated or felt helplessness while caring for their newborn. Every time Isabella became overwhelmed, Paul withdrew from her.

"Precisely when I needed him most, he would disappear," she explained. "It was then I realized that while I'd avoided marrying my father, I'd actually married someone very much like my mom. She never faced anything. Running away was her way of coping with anything unpleasant."

Soon, Isabella's expressive nature became a constant source of conflict in her marriage. This brought her to a place of high anxiety, fearing that Paul would leave her like her mother had. And that's what eventually happened. As Isabella's fear grew, so did her desperation for Paul to stay. The more assurance she demanded, the more he pulled away. Paul began staying at work later, going out without her, and refusing to help her with parenting.

"The divorce itself was horrible. If I weren't holding it together for my daughter, I think I would have just gone to bed forever. I didn't want to live my life without Paul."

Isabella had every intention of having an "until death do us part" kind of marriage. She was devastated when Paul moved out of their home and in with another woman. "I lost Paul and felt exactly like I did when my mother left me. I felt utterly rejected."

"Isabella, even though it felt the same as your mother leaving, the end of your marriage was quite different," I pointed out.

Isabella looked shocked. "What do you mean? They both left me!"

"Yes, they did. But your mother left you when you were a child. She violated her responsibility as your mother. When your marriage ended, you were an adult."

She persisted. "But didn't Paul violate his responsibility as my husband?"

I nodded. "Yes, he did, but ending a relationship with another adult is quite a different dynamic than abandoning a child. The trauma you suffered as a child has become your core wound."

After a moment of thought, a light came into her eyes. "Yes, I can see that. My core wound."

"Paul's hurtful action triggered the enormous pain of your childhood," I continued. "Your survival was actually threatened when you were a child. Essentially you were left under the supervision of a father who was incapable of dealing with his own life, and a brother who was a child himself."

Her eyes filled with tears. "It was horrible."

"Yes, but when your marriage ended, you were not a child. You were a grown woman. It was awful; it was painful. No one wants to suffer like that. But there's a huge difference. Do you see that?"

Isabella let out a huge sigh. "Yes, intellectually, at any rate. Both were excruciating."

Having gone through my own divorce, I had a good idea of what Isabella had experienced. "Of course, both were painful. But the divorce felt even more painful because it stirred up your childhood core wound. You were triggered. And that's why it hurt so much when Paul walked out the door."

Isabella's First Trigger: Jack Not Calling When He Promised

Most people are triggered at various points in their lives. The more severe the past trauma, the more severe the reaction often is. As time passed for Isabella, she adapted to single life better than she expected. "The more time I was away from Paul, the better I felt about myself," she shared. "He really wasn't good for me, and quite honestly, I'm better off without him.

"I'm a supplier for a chain of clothing shops, and I became friends with one of our buyers. Sarah had gone through a divorce too. She invited me to a divorce recovery support group, and it was so wonderful for me. I met so many people who were going through the same thing I was, and I figured if they could survive it, so could I. Plus, there were men there, so I dated a few guys. I've been emotionally strong for a few years now, and I've always been the one who ended it. But then I met Jack."

Isabella put her face in her hands. "Now look at me. I'm a basket case." By the third day of Jack's trip, she was triggered, and feelings of rejection tore through her with such a vengeance that they terrified her. Her intense reaction to not receiving a call from Jack revived deeply rooted fears of being alone and rejected—the same feelings she had when her mother left and then amplified when her marriage ended. She had lost two people very close to her, and those losses were extremely painful.

> *When we're triggered, we're not reacting to the situation in the present but to a traumatic experience in our past.*

I explained to her that when we're triggered, we're not reacting to the situation in the present but to a traumatic experience in our past. Before her marriage ended, her ex-husband often failed to call when he promised. The silence had been a sign that her marriage was ending. Isabella was reliving her divorce and other serious disappointments in her past.

Was Jack the same kind of man Paul had turned out to be? Jack said he would call, and he didn't. What did this mean to Jack? Did his business trip hit a huge snag? Was he extremely tired and busy? Was Jack rethinking his relationship and losing interest? Or did he simply forget? Isabella had no idea what his silence meant. But she realized a man's silence was a trigger for her.

Isabella's Second Trigger: Beginning to Feel Deeply Attached

We have many types of relationships in which we "fall in love"—with our children, our parents, our closest friends, and our partners. The experience of falling in love often generates intense feelings of belonging and connection. Love can be euphoric, causing us to feel enormous happiness and joy. At the same time, these intense connections can generate the fear of overwhelming vulnerability and potential loss.

Isabella was emotionally overcome by the depth of her feelings toward Jack. The prospect of being close to someone new seemed far more dangerous now than it had a few days prior. Isabella linked love with feelings of insecurity, danger, and horrible pain. The more attached she became, the more confused and scared she felt. She was afraid this man could reactivate her core wound once again.

Step Three: Describe Your Patterns of Self-Sabotage

As we've discussed, when we feel in danger, the amygdala or fear center is activated. When this happens, powerful hormones like adrenaline flood our systems; blood is drawn toward our extremities so we can act quickly in response to danger. We have only three options—to fight, flee, or freeze. That's it.

Our amygdala has no concept of time whatsoever. The amygdala cannot differentiate between experiences of the past or present, or worries about the future. The amygdala knows only one reality: right now. This is why when you are triggered, you reexperience the past trauma as if it were happening in the present—with all of the pain you felt the first time around.

This leaves us little chance of maintaining perspective, recognizing nuance, or seeing the situation from another point

But when you are triggered, your reaction is out of proportion to the event.

of view. So we overreact by 1) becoming overly aggressive or demanding (fight), 2) running away or cutting off relationships abruptly (flee), or 3) refusing to talk, zoning out, and dissociating (freeze). Any and all of these turn out to be extremely poor strategies for long-term, healthy relationships.

We see all three types of responses in Isabella's family.

1. Fight: Isabella was a fighter. She tried to keep her mother from leaving. She begged Paul not to leave, trying everything she could imagine to save their marriage.
2. Flee: Her mother and her brother were the type of people who ran away from conflict. Her mother took off for London instead of dealing with her current marriage. Isabella's brother left home at seventeen and never settled down.
3. Freeze: Isabella's father shut down and refused to face difficult situations. He isolated himself, turning into a bitter man who let life pass him by.

All of these actions are appropriate in genuinely dangerous situations. But when you are triggered, your reaction grows out of proportion to the event. Adopting these reflexes as a way of life, results in patterns of self-sabotage. It's next to impossible to build a healthy relationship when you're perpetually running away, becoming aggressive, or freezing up and cutting off communication. Often, once you calm down, you can see that you behaved inappropriately. But for many, it can take a long time to recognize these patterns.

Self-Sabotage Pattern One: Aggressively Defending Herself Against Imagined Abandonment

I asked Isabella, "When Jack didn't call, what was your first reaction?"

She smiled sheepishly. "I used to call my ex and leave long, hateful voice messages about how he had let me down and couldn't be trusted. When I reached for the phone to leave Jack the same kind of message, I knew I was about to ruin whatever could come of this new love. So that's why I called you."

"You wanted to take some kind of protective action?"

She nodded. "Yes. I didn't want to sit, waiting like my dad who pathetically let my mother leave without a fight. I called Sarah, though, hoping she would understand."

"But she didn't?"

"Not exactly. She said, 'Don't let this guy get to you, Isabella. If he's not trustworthy, kick him to the curb.'"

"She has also gone through a divorce, right?"

Isabella nodded again. "Yes. In some ways, hers was actually much worse than mine. She and her husband were in business together, and she found out he had been siphoning off thousands of dollars into a secret account. And he wasn't even having an affair. He just wanted to act richer than he was in front of his friends. By the time she figured it out, it was already too late. The money was gone. She lost her home and had to file for bankruptcy during the divorce."

"So how does it feel for your friend not to understand?"

She shrugged. "It's just the way she is, I guess. She has landed on her feet like a cat with nine lives. She started a new business, this time in design, which is how I met her. In about two years, she's already one of the most successful designers in the area. Her gripe was that she'd been fooled by him. She said, 'Oh, my ex is just like my father—always lying. I thought I was smarter than that.'"

I smiled. "I get it now. Your friend has a different type of core wound. She was wounded by someone who lied to her, so she doesn't react the same way you do. She didn't experience her divorce as rejection because she didn't feel rejected by her father. Instead, she was angry with herself, and with you, for being tricked."

A slow smile came across her face. "Yes, that makes sense. The trigger is based on my experiences. Is that right?"

"Yes. So what kind of things do you say to yourself when you're triggered?"

"Well, that I'm a loser. That I won't ever have a successful relationship with a man. That Jack is just like everyone else I've cared about. That, sooner or later, he will leave me too."

I pointed out that when we're triggered, we often tell ourselves scary and hateful things. Here are some examples of negative self-talk I've heard from my clients:

- I always pick the wrong people to love.
- Why even try when everyone disappoints me?
- I'm too broken to find love.
- I can't survive someone else leaving me.
- Why can't I stop this pattern?

We react to being triggered by engaging in negative self-talk. In turn, negative self-talk exacerbates our fear. The dynamic is cyclical. Everything feels like it's life or death, kill or be killed, survival or destruction. Pay attention to the way you talk to yourself to see if you're using extreme words like "always," "everyone," or "can't survive." There's no truth to these words—only fear.

When we act out of fear—without compassion, insight, or reason—someone typically gets hurt. You might mistreat someone you love or sabotage a relationship. In fact, you often end up hurting yourself. Isabella's fear was that she would end up alone. If she repeated her self-sabotaging patterns, she would unwittingly bring that upon herself.

Self-Sabotage Pattern Two: Fleeing from the Situation Before She Can Get Hurt

Isabella told me she also had the impulse to call Jack and end the relationship. "When Paul left me, I swore to myself I'd never allow any man to do that to me again. That was Sarah's advice. She said, 'Be the one who breaks up. Don't let him dump you.'"

"So if you broke up with him, you'd avoid him breaking up with you?"
She nodded.

When I asked her to let me know more of the negative thoughts she had been telling herself, she responded:

- "Only a fool would let another man leave her."
- "He'll never get to see me cry."
- "I want to punish him for breaking his promise to call."
- "Who does he think he is? He's nobody."
- "I don't care about Jack anyway."

"But what do you really want?" I asked her.

Her eyes filled with tears again. "I really want this to work out, if possible. I want to find out if Jack is the kind of guy I can trust and if we could have a future."

"So ending the relationship just to avoid rejection is the opposite of what you truly want?"

"Not the best strategy, is it?"

"No," I said. "When we act out of our fear, we seldom get what we want or need."

Step Four: Imagine the Worst-Case Scenario

Isabella falsely believed that experiencing another rejection could kill her. When we struggle with issues of rejection, we are most often trying to avoid feeling vulnerable. It's easy to equate being vulnerable with being unprotected. But true vulnerability is based in the strength that comes from knowing and trusting ourselves.

When in a rational place, when her frontal lobe was activated, Isabella knew she would not literally die if Jack ended the relationship. But when caught in the fear trap of rejection, she felt and thought like a young girl who was, once again, being abandoned by her mother. Stuck in the fear trap, she lost access to her adult ability to care for and protect herself.

When we act out of our fear, we seldom get what we want or need.

Negative Self-Talk

Our feelings can easily influence how we think and act—if we give them that power. However, it can also work the other way around. We can choose thoughts and actions that redirect our emotions to a healthy place. Cognitive behavioral therapy (CBT), which I integrated into my approach, focuses on changing the way we think and behave in order to change our emotions. If we think negative thoughts about ourselves and others, we are likely to feel critical and uncomfortable. If we think positive thoughts, we are more likely to feel comfortable and content. Experts believe that negative thoughts, and the resulting chemicals they release in the brain, contribute to depression, anxiety, and unhappiness. By choosing what you will focus your thoughts on, you have more power than you might realize.

If left uninterrupted, negative self-talk will keep you from calming down and keep you trapped in the amygdala. Below are four types of self-defeating mind chatter:

- Negative self-talk is verbal and/or internal dialogue that demoralizes and discourages us.
- Negative automatic thoughts are counterproductive thoughts that arise automatically when a situation triggers emotional discomfort.
- Irrational beliefs are illogical and highly limiting conclusions that our mind takes as truth.
- Catastrophizing thoughts are the persistent, irrational worries over an extremely unlikely worst-case scenario.

Together, Isabella and I faced her worst fear trap—that Jack would leave her. I instructed her to describe how she felt as if it were really happening in the present tense. "I imagine that Jack returns from his trip, never calls me again, and blows me off with no real explanation."

"What would happen if you never heard from Jack again?"

"I'd be devastated, and I'd want to demand that he talk to me."

"What would happen if he refused?"

"I'd be angry and hurt. It would be awful."

"Do you have any other fears about what might happen?"

Isabella nodded. "I can imagine him eventually calling and making excuses. But he would have lost interest in the relationship. He would have already checked out."

"How would that feel?"

"Well, like I'd been abandoned and rejected again."

"Anything else?"

"If we broke up, I could imagine running into him. We live in the same neighborhood. I would hate to walk into a restaurant while he was having a romantic dinner with another woman."

"What would that feel like?"

She looked down. "I'd feel humiliated."

"Can you survive feeling humiliated?"

She glared at me. "Well, I wouldn't want to."

"I understand that you don't want to experience this emotional pain. But could you *survive* it?"

"Well, of course I could." She stopped and realized what she'd just said. "I could survive this ending, couldn't I?"

"Yes, you could. At this point, you don't know if he is trustworthy or not. But the key to feeling safe is trusting yourself. If you have confidence in yourself, then you'll retain your personal power and be able to handle anything."

"Wow, I've never thought of safety in that way."

I pressed in on that point. "If Jack never speaks to you again, you will see the kind of man he is. But how he behaves defines him, not you. *You* define who you are."

She nodded. "I can see this now. I will trust myself regardless of whatever Jack does. If Jack runs away from relationships, I'll know he's like my mother and brother. And if he has already checked out, I'll know he's like my father—someone I can't trust."

"That's right."

"And I think it would be wise for me to slow down a bit," Isabella said. "I'm moving too fast when I don't know if Jack is trustworthy or not. The fact that I have been so fearful tells me I'm not properly protecting myself."

She sat back in her chair with a sense of self-confidence. "I can deal with this. I'm strong enough now."

Isabella imagined the worst possible thing that could happen, and to her surprise, she didn't die. In fact, she was sitting in front of me, alive and well, with a new sense of personal power. I asked her to describe the most likely scenarios: Jack could end the relationship—which she could survive; she might end the relationship—if she discovers Jack has a pattern of breaking his promises; or they could build a healthy, long-term relationship.

The future was still open to Isabella. She had much more power in the shaping the future than she had imagined. That's because adults have more power than children.

Step Five: Create a Courageous Brain

I know firsthand that living in fear, whatever the fear might be, is not an easy pattern to break. When we fall into a fear trap, our instinctive drive for protection is strong. We feel driven to control what will happen. The problem is that we can't control anything or anyone but ourselves. The more positive neuropathways we create, the more courageous our brains become. The more we repeat these exercises, the more we are able to accept our vulnerabilities while feeling safe.

As we began the focused meditation together, I asked Isabella to remember two experiences from her past. The first was a time she felt safe and loved. Isabella recalled that her father whistled when he was happy. After her mother left, the whistling became an infrequent occurrence. However, he came home whistling once while Isabella was in high school. At that time, her father was happy. At least for that moment, Isabella felt safe. That evening, she and her dad had a joyful meal together, and she fell asleep watching television with him. Recalling this memory, Isabella smiled, taking comfort in the feelings the memory evoked.

Next, I asked her to remember a time she felt rejected by someone in a small way that didn't mean a great deal to her. "Don't focus on a time when you were deeply wounded. Think of a time you felt slighted by someone."

. . . .
You need to feel it before you can heal it.
. . . .

She told me about a time when her father had promised to pick her up after school and take her to buy new shoes. "He never showed up. I felt rejected, of course, and I walked home feeling awful. I still remember being upset with him. When he got home, he apologized. That made a big difference to me—that he actually said he was sorry."

"That's a good one to start with—a memory of rejection but not something extremely hurtful. We're going to work up to the harder memories."

Why did I ask her to do this? Because we spend so much time invalidating ourselves, suppressing our emotions, and/or blaming others. We do this to avoid feeling the true weight of our pain. Even in traditional therapy, we often talk and talk around our wounds while being totally detached from our emotions. We fear we won't be able to survive or cope if we confront them. And it's true that these emotions can even put us in physical discomfort—like tense shoulders, a headache, or a knot in our stomach. They may make us restless; our minds racing to solve the problem that triggered us.

Here's the amazing thing: When we give ourselves permission to really feel our emotions, we can begin to move past them. Over time, your brain will begin to calm down and realize that the event that *feels like it's happening now* is actually in your past. This is important. You have already survived this memory. It's over and done with. And you are still standing! All that remains is the memory etched in your brain and the chemicals this memory triggers.

That realization can be intensely satisfying on both an emotional and physiological level, releasing hormones that bring us pleasure and a sense of well-being. Your brain becomes desensitized to the chemicals behind the fear, and the new hormones form a new, positive neuropathway. We then focus back on the positive truths that strengthen that healthy path. In summation, we feel and validate, we realize we can survive, and we move forward.

Focused Meditation Exercise:

Before you start this fifteen-minute meditation, select an extremely happy moment when you felt accepted and loved without question. Then choose a memory of when you experienced a sense of rejection without being triggered in a significant way. Once you have those memories ready in your mind, you can begin.

Escape the Fear Trap of Being Rejected
Begin

Start by getting into a comfortable position with your arms and legs uncrossed. Breathe in through your nose and exhale through your mouth. You may be breathing shallowly, primarily from your chest, but focus your attention on breathing deeply into your abdomen. It may take a while to relax to the point where your stomach expands and retracts with each slow breath. Continue to breathe in through your nose and out through your mouth.

5-Minute Mark

Now that you are more relaxed, think of one experience in your life when you felt accepted and secure. You might have experienced this with a special person or in a group by feeling like you belonged. Think of this experience as you breathe in and out. Use all of your senses to describe what you saw, felt, smelled, and heard. Experience it as fully as possible. Sit with this memory and allow yourself to feel at peace, loved, and accepted.

8-Minute Mark

Turn your attention to an experience when you felt slighted or mildly rejected. Again, this experience could involve one or more people. Perhaps you felt singled out or embarrassed among a group of your friends. Use all your senses to describe what you saw, felt, smelled, and heard. Experience it as fully as possible. Sit with this memory and allow yourself to feel uncomfortable and unaccepted. Don't shy away from it; embrace it fully.

When you notice your negative feelings are fading, you will know that your brain has become desensitized to this memory. Set your timer for the twelve-minute mark. If the feelings continue to be strong, then repeat this meditation tomorrow with the same memory. Continue to use this experience until the intense emotional response fades.

12-Minute Mark

Shift your focus back to the positive memory you chose for this exercise. Return to the place where you felt totally loved and accepted. Make this memory as real as possible. Feel the clothes on your body. Smell the fragrance in the air. If you were eating, recall the taste of the food. Listen to the voices and the laughter. Take in the kindness shown to you.

14-Minute Mark

Now wiggle your fingers and toes and slowly bring yourself back to the present. Take a few more deep breaths. You are now ready to engage in your life with a deeper conviction that you are safe and at peace.

15-Minute Mark

You have been changed through this meditation. While you may not have come to a place where your brain is completely desensitized to this memory, your brain has been soothed. The energy level in the fear center of your brain has decreased, and your frontal lobe has been stimulated.

If this meditation is helpful to you, I recommend you repeat it with memories that increase in emotional intensity. If a memory is too painful or upsetting, it's best to seek out a therapist who can be with you through the process. The goal is to become desensitized, not overwhelmed. When we gain control over our fearful memories, our brains begin rewiring our neuropathways.

Step Six: Live Free of the Fear Trap

Most of us enter new experiences or relationships with some optimism believing that whatever hurt we experienced in the past will not be repeated. When we stumble into our fear trap, however, we find ourselves back in a sad, familiar place. Behaviors and attitudes that protected you in the past may now be sabotaging your chances for success, happiness, and intimacy. The starting place is acknowledging that, once again, we're overreacting and repeating a self-defeating pattern.

Isabella took a very important step by realizing she was on the verge of making the same mistakes she'd made in the past. Her anxiety tempted her to repeat a pattern of behavior that ultimately did not give her the happiness she desired. If she did not care about a man, she remained in control of herself and her emotions. But once she felt a strong attraction, she abruptly became dependent and demanding. She told me, "I'm clearly overreacting, but I can't seem to stop myself."

I assured her that everyone is triggered at some point, and it's nothing to be ashamed of. What's important is to recognize as soon as possible that you've been triggered, minimizing overreaction and hurting or confusing others. On an emotional level, Isabella confused Jack with her ex-husband, Paul. Any action she took that treated Jack as if he were Paul could have sabotaged her possible future with Jack.

She processed the situation with her frontal lobe and had a variety of insights—something that was impossible inside of her fear center. "I blamed Paul for the divorce when it happened," she said. "I didn't see how I played a role in it at all. But over time, through the divorce recovery support group, I realized I did play a role in my divorce. The angrier and more desperate I became, the more Paul pulled away."

When we fear rejection, it is hard to trust others. Most importantly, we don't trust ourselves. When triggered, we're cut off from adult functioning. We can only deal with the situation when we regain access to our frontal lobes. When we are calm, we discover that we can rely on ourselves to handle just about anything that comes our way.

We discussed positive statements she could say to herself to replace the critical voice she often heard in her head:

- I trust myself, and I can survive no matter what happens in this relationship.
- I am learning how to protect myself when I'm in a relationship.
- When I'm triggered and thrown into extreme fear, I have ways to calm down.
- I deserve to be loved by someone who is capable and trustworthy.
- I can keep my emotions in check while I learn more about Jack.

For long-term relationships to succeed, both people must trust themselves to manage intimacy and trust that the other is capable of partnership. Learning to trust ourselves does not mean becoming naïve. Genuine trust actually allows us to release what we have no control over and accept reality. This is the pivotal first step in moving from a life lived in a fear trap to one of resilience, self-confidence, and courage.

As the trust that Isabella had in herself grew, Jack calling or not no longer seemed like a life-or-death issue. She knew she could rely on herself to handle whatever happened in the relationship. She recognized she didn't have to trust Jack to feel safe within herself. Of course, she needed to find out if Jack was a trustworthy person before she invested more into the relationship, but she first needed to trust she could handle whatever came of this or any other romance.

Isabella and I met for about six more months as she continued her daily meditation. She decided to step back from her relationship with Jack for a while. She realized that she needed time to focus on herself and develop a stronger resilience when she was triggered. Regardless of who she would date, and perhaps eventually marry, she knew it was her responsibility to create a safe world for herself.

Key Points

- As children, we needed adults to build strong emotional connections with us.
- We also needed adult role models to show us how to communicate difficult emotions and resolve conflict.
- Without proper role models, we can grow into adulthood without knowing how to communicate our most vulnerable emotions and needs.
- In our adult relationships, triggers from our childhood wounds can cause us to overreact.
- Some triggers are particularly strong if people are traumatized in their childhood and then retraumatized in a similar way as adults.
- Because everyone has experienced some kind of difficulty in the past, anyone can become triggered. There's no shame in it.
- Strong emotions, even if they seem positive (such as love or attraction), can become triggers if they make us feel vulnerable to being hurt or rejected.
- People in the fear trap of rejection will fight, flee, or freeze, which often causes hurt to themselves and others rather than giving them what they really want.
- People in this fear trap often use extreme words such as "always/never," "should/shouldn't," "good/bad," or "all/nothing" because they cannot access their frontal lobe to see other perspectives.
- When trapped by fear, you may describe yourself or others in extremely degrading ways with words like "stupid," "idiot," "worthless," and so on.

- When we realize we're overreacting because we're triggered, we can prevent ourselves from perpetuating patterns of self-sabotage and build healthy relationships.
- One of the most powerful things we can do when we're triggered is simply feel the emotions but not act on them. Our brains will get desensitized, and we'll naturally feel better.

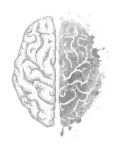

FEAR TRAP THREE

Are You Afraid of Confrontation?

Any psychologist will tell you that healing comes from honest
confrontation with our injury . . . until we face it head on,
we will have issues moving forward in a healthy way.
—*Nate Parker*

Randy was the epitome of a seasoned, professional real estate agent. His parents immigrated to the United States from Costa Rica when Randy was nine. Now in his mid-forties, Randy's classic blue suit and perfectly matched tie gave him an air of polished refinement. Randy had first come to me while he was launching his career and was intimidated by the intense competition with other agents. He and I worked on distinguishing between aggression and assertion, and he found his niche in the market.

It was always nice to see his photo on "for sale" signs all over our community. Randy had become one of the most successful realtors in the area, but one day, he called and said he needed a "refresher course on standing up for myself." I was happy to see him again.

Step One: Tell Your Story

"Dr. Stella, I started a new venture that hasn't gone as well as I'd hoped," Randy said after sitting down across from me. "I've been quite successful in selling homes for couples looking to downsize after raising their families, and even though I've sold so many houses, my wife, Dalia and I haven't bought one for ourselves. As you may remember, my wife is an interior designer. We've been waiting for just the right property, and to be honest, we want a really nice home.

"Dalia and I decided we could expand both our businesses together. We took a seminar on how to buy older homes, fix them up, and resell them. I know real estate, and Dalia knows interior design, but neither of us has had any experience in construction or architectural design. As we were listening to the presenter, we agreed this was something we wanted to do, but we both realized we needed to team up with someone else, maybe another couple.

"During the break, we met this charming couple named Matt and Kate. They were just what we were looking for—or so we thought. She is a realtor as well, and Matt is a contractor. He said he knew architects if we needed one, and added, 'Kate is rather humble, but she can swing a hammer with the best of them. She can help out with the work itself.'"

Randy explained to me how the two couples jumped right into the project. "Our plan fell so easily into place. Kate and I worked together to find a fixer-upper with great potential for a high resale price. Dalia and I would live in it during the remodel to save money on rent for the project. While Dalia and I were at work during the day, Matt would act as the contractor, and Kate would help on the smaller jobs to hold down labor costs. We thought it would take us six months to finish the remodel, and then we'd put it on the market. We'd share the expenses and split the profit. If it worked out, we'd make it an ongoing business arrangement."

"That sounds like an exciting opportunity," I said. "But the fact that you're here makes me think it didn't work out as planned?"

"Not at all! We moved into the fixer a year and a half ago. We're an entire year past the deadline. Matt and Kate get to go back to their nice home at the end of the day. We, on the other hand, are stuck in this pit. It's all so chaotic."

"What's the holdup?"

"Matt is a perfectionist to such an extreme degree that nothing is ever good enough. He'll almost finish a tile job or complete the cabinet installation, and then say, 'This isn't any good' and pull it apart to start over. Kate always sides with him. I think their work is fantastic, and I tell them so. I've bent over backward to be supportive and complimentary, but it's nearly impossible for the two of them to finish anything. Dalia and I have been living in sawdust and half-completed rooms for all of this time. Our marriage is suffering because my wife thinks I need to take a stronger stand with them. She says, 'Randy, they could have built the Taj Mahal in this time.'"

"That sounds really hard. How do you feel about the situation?"

A look of anger washed across his face. "It's taking everything I've got not to fly into a rage. I'm furious with myself for getting into this mess. I'm so tired of my wife nagging me. And Matt and Kate are ridiculous. I have a list of grievances with them a mile long."

"Have you and your wife talked with Matt and Kate about this?"

He sighed. "We've tried to. Dalia just sits and smolders, first angry with them and then angry with me for not drawing a line in the sand."

"Dalia doesn't speak for herself?"

Randy smiled sheepishly. "You haven't met my wife, Dr. Stella. She is more than capable of saying what's on her mind. But I have asked her to let me handle this because I don't want to burn any bridges with Kate. She is a very well-respected realtor, and if she wanted to tarnish my reputation, she could quite easily."

I nodded. "So Dalia holds her tongue but isn't happy with how you are handling the situation."

"Dalia's not happy with anybody involved, especially me."

Smiling, I pointed out, "It doesn't sound like you're very happy with the other three either."

He shook his head. "To make things worse, Matt gets into arguments with the city and has yet

Are you afraid you'll fly into a rage if you start talking about your feelings?

to pass an inspection. So much of what he has done on the house doesn't have proper permits. But before anything gets finished, he finds fault with some aspect of the build. He's very hard to get along with.

"I've dropped hints to Matt and Kate about the length of time this has taken. I encourage them to work a little faster or give suggestions that might speed up the process. But the more I try to get them to go faster, the more they push back. Matt will say, 'I have my own reputation to be concerned about. If I do a shoddy job on this house, who will hire me after this is over?' Kate agrees and says, 'Why don't you support us rather than undermine us? We're creating an amazing house that will sell for much more if we use the best materials with the highest craftsmanship. Don't you have any standards?'"

Randy ran his hands over his face. "When they start blaming us—well, that's when Dalia stands up and excuses herself, saying she needs to get back to work. Basically, we have one bedroom without a finished closet, one bathroom with a flushing toilet and a tub without a shower head, and part of a kitchen; just enough to prepare basic meals. After a year and a half! But the rest of the house is in various stages of disrepair. We're living illegally in this unfinished space, and I'm the bad guy in everyone's eyes."

"You sound pretty angry about this, but you haven't directly confronted anyone about it yet," I said. "Are you afraid you'll fly into a rage if you start talking about your feelings?"

He nodded his head. "Yes, and that would freak everyone out. No one has seen me really lose my temper. It's not pretty." He paused. "And what if they get furious with us? What if they abandon us in this mess? I don't know anything about remodeling. We can't afford to finish this on our own.

"Dalia and I work hard all day and want to come home to a place that we can sell as soon as possible. But my wife gets upset when she comes home and finds Matt ripping out the electrical circuit he just put in, while Kate strokes his ego and praises his high standards. It's such a mess. I may lose my investment, my career, and my wife."

Step Two: Identify Your Triggers

I assured Randy that his fears were not imaginary. If the situation didn't change, it could very well get worse. But he was right that exploding in rage wouldn't help anyone.

"Randy, where in your past did you learn to handle your anger this way?" I asked.

He thought about that for a moment. "Well, I guess when I was a kid. It reminds me of feeling trapped within my chaotic family."

I knew from our previous work that Randy grew up in a small town in North Central Ohio as the oldest of five.

"My house was filled with extended family—aunts, uncles, grandparents, cousins—plus my siblings. It was loud, with everyone talking at the same time. I'm a quiet person, myself, and I withdrew from the chaos."

"What were your parents like?"

"My mother was in charge, like a general trying to organize the army of relatives that marched through our house on a daily basis. Most of the time, she was wonderful. She loved having people around. But every so often, she'd get angry, and then watch out! She scared all of us. If we did something wrong, she'd slap us. If she really got mad, she'd take a belt to us. When my mom got into one of these states, I was helpless.

"My dad never stood up for us. He'd see her go after one of us, and he'd just disappear. I had no one to help me. He would withdraw and refuse to speak to anyone for days at a time. When he shut her out, my mother would fuss over him, trying to regain his attention—back to her kind self. But after a while, she'd blow up at him for being so avoidant. I never wanted to lose my temper with anyone like she did."

Observing how uncomfortable he had become, I said, "I'll bet you tried to keep on her good side."

He smiled. "I just wanted to go under the radar. I never expressed my feelings if they might have made someone upset. To save money, I went to a local junior college and then right into real estate after that. I just didn't want to bother my parents with extra stress, so I tried to make a good living as soon as possible."

The Past Is Not the Problem

Two people can experience the same event yet have radically different reactions and interpretations. Our perception of an event in our lives is often different than what actually happened. First, we only saw a partial piece of the event—from our point of view. Second, the piece we saw was colored by all our past experiences. That means we might assign a meaning to an event that doesn't exist at all for anyone else. As a result, our perceptions of events bias our feelings and thoughts toward them.

Therefore, when processing the past, what actually happened is not as important as your experience of what happened. Indeed, no one has perfect recall, as we experience the same event from different physical and emotional viewpoints. But our experiences are recorded in our brains, and impact our lives in the present. Accurate or inaccurate historically, the way we interpret those memories drives our future habits and triggers.

"Did you ever confront your parents about what happened?"

Randy's eyes grew dark with anger. "Yes, I did—I had just moved out of town, but I came back for Thanksgiving. The whole family was there. We got done eating, and everyone got up to go sit in the family room. But then my mom yelled out to me and my brother Stuart.

"She goes, 'Oh, no you don't, you two! You're on kitchen duty!' And then she starts going on about how we need to make ourselves useful, how we never do anything to help, how we're not around enough.

"She kept going on, putting down my accomplishments and treating me like a kid. My brother nudged me to come on. I'm usually really calm, but the more she insulted me, the more I felt this rage building up. I turned to my mom and told her I was a grown man now with my own career and my own income. I actually raised my voice. I shouted, 'You can't just smack me around like when I was a kid, you have to treat me like an adult now.'

"That was what really set her off. Everyone went quiet in the other room. She started shouting back at me, asking me who I thought I was. I was so mad I was shaking. My mother shook with rage when she snarled, 'Get out of my house. Now!'

My brother grabbed me by the arm and pulled me out. We didn't hear anyone say a word until we were all the way to the car on the street. That's when I started to realize I'd just blown up at her like she did with me. I didn't come back to visit for several months. When I came back, everyone acted like it never happened."

Randy threw up his hands. "What did I expect? That my mother would suddenly admit that she was wrong? No, it was foolish to have tried. And what was my solution? To blow up at my own mom? No. I decided that if my only choice is to become mean like her or stuff my feelings and keep the peace like my dad had, then I was going to follow in my father's footsteps."

Randy had resigned himself to avoid the slightest bit of conflict because it triggered such terrifying memories. He didn't want anyone to be angry with him, and he was afraid that if he ever got angry again, he'd lose control over his emotions. Randy held the faulty belief that if no one got angry, he would be safe, and the family would be at peace. So, when conflict was on the horizon, Randy never asserted himself. Like his father, he withdrew from confronting anyone or expressing his own feelings of displeasure.

Randy's First Trigger: The Threat of Other People's Anger

"I understand that there's a lot of anger between you and your mother," I said, "but what does that have to do with what is happening in this remodeling situation? It's not getting better by avoiding the tension."

Randy smiled sadly. "I have really painted myself into a corner. There's no way I can win here. I'm trying to keep Matt and my wife from blowing up at each other. Kate takes Matt's side, while everyone gets angrier at me. I get so freaked out."

It's critical to take ownership of our own wounds and self-destructive patterns from our youth. If we don't, it's possible for us to recreate them in our adult life. As a boy, Randy was trapped by his mother's temper and his father's passivity. Now he allowed this same dynamic to occur, even though he was grown. He didn't yet realize that he had more power and options than he had when he was younger.

Randy's Second Trigger: Fear of His Own Mishandled Anger

As his best efforts to keep the peace failed, Randy was feeling increasingly resentful and angry about the situation. As a people pleaser who didn't like conflict, he was further horrified by the anger that was growing inside of him. What would happen if he lost it? He didn't want to hurt anyone, but he was at the end of his rope. He saw only two options—be abusive like his mother or passive like his father.

"I don't ever want someone to be afraid of me like I feared my mom," he told me. "I'm afraid that one day I'll just lose it and lash out at all of them. That is my biggest fear."

I asked Randy to tell me about the harsh things he was saying to himself. He grinned and said, "You know about that?"

I nodded. "When we are trapped in fear, we often say nasty and hurtful things to ourselves."

"Oh, I have a lot of them," he said, listing a few. "You are just like your mother underneath. You will hurt people if you don't stuff down your feelings. You want to be an abuser? You want to ruin your marriage? Keep that door shut, or else you'll lose everything."

"That's a long list you have there," "I observed. "But we can interrupt that negative self-talk. You'll be amazed at how different your life will be when you do."

> It's critical to take ownership of our own wounds and self-destructive patterns from our youth. If we don't, it's possible for us to recreate them in our adult life.

Step Three: Describe Patterns of Self-Sabotage

Randy learned that when we allow ourselves to be controlled by our unconscious fears, we engage in actions that actually manifest the exact outcomes we want so desperately to avoid. In his effort to avoid conflict, Randy created situations where conflict could not be dealt with in a healthy way.

But none of us can avoid conflict and have authentic relationships. All relationships involve misunderstandings and challenges. These can be addressed peacefully or mishandled and allowed to fester into a destructive force. Randy had two self-defeating strategies when faced with normal conflict in relationships.

Self-Sabotage Pattern One: Blocking Honest Communication About Conflict

Because Randy's mother was unable to control her anger, Randy feared all expressions of conflict. He tried to silence Dalia by making her promise not to say anything to Matt and Kate. Dalia wasn't like Randy's mother. She was able to express her displeasure without exploding in rage. But Randy was overly sensitive to any display of unhappiness. It felt too threatening to him. Asking Dalia not to speak for herself only added to the overall dysfunction of the relationship.

Self-Sabotage Pattern Two: Blaming Others for All the Problems

Matt had a hard time dealing effectively with other people, as demonstrated by the antagonistic relationship he developed with the city inspectors. Granted, the hostility may have been shared by the inspectors. It's extremely rare for one person to hold all the blame, while the other is completely innocent of miscommunication. However, the fact remained that they did not have the needed permits for construction after a year and a half.

Randy used Matt's issues to defend his own avoidance. If Randy hadn't been so intimidated by the prospect of honest communication, he may have assisted Matt when dealing with the city and other licensing agencies. Instead, Randy pulled away and left Matt to handle this part of the problem on his own. This further exacerbated the conflict and Randy's fear of a blowup.

Step Four: Imagine the Worst-Case Scenario

Anger is not a comfortable emotion for any of us. Those who have been caught in the fear trap of confrontation, however, view anger as life-threatening. Randy was going to great lengths to avoid conflict of any kind. I asked him a simple question: "Is avoiding conflict bringing peace to your life?"

Randy chuckled sadly. "No, not at all. But neither has confronting people. Look at how my parents refused to admit I was ever abused."

I explained that it's easy for us to get caught up in the details of the past when we have such strong emotions tied to them. "You don't need your parents to admit anything. Your brain has recorded the emotional memories. That's what is true for you. While it can feel satisfying to have someone else affirm our experiences, it's not necessary in order to break free from our fear traps."

Randy let out a deep breath. "That is so encouraging to me. I don't have to get them to admit it?"

I shook my head. "You aren't a little boy any longer. You are a grown man, but you're setting yourself up to repeat your worst fears. What will happen if you continue your pattern of conflict avoidance?"

"Well, it isn't working. It's impossible to make everyone happy."

"What is the worst thing that could happen to you right now?"

Randy paused before responding. "Matt and Kate could get angry and quit the project. They could leave me and Dalia with

> *While it can feel satisfying to have someone else affirm our experiences, it's not necessary in order to break free from a fear trap.*

the entire mess—the house payment that we share, the materials and contractors we both pay for. I don't know if they'd demand to be bought out or what damage they could do."

"Is that the worst thing about the business partnership you can imagine?" I asked.

"No, the worst thing would be if they walked away from the project and then sued us for their part of the investment. That would be the worst thing I could imagine."

"What would happen if they walked away and then sued you?"

Randy stared at me as if I'd lost my mind. "Why ask me that?"

"Because I want to help you see how resilient you are." I sat back for a moment and took a good look at him. "It doesn't seem to me like you are breathing very deeply."

Randy took a deep gasp of air. "No, I was holding my breath."

"Yes, that's what we all do when we are being controlled by the fear center in our brains. We stop breathing. Let's pause for a moment so you can calm yourself down."

Randy took about five deep breaths. "I feel better now. I can tell the difference."

"Yes, the simple act of breathing can move us out of a fear trap and into a place where we can have a clearer perspective on the problem. So let's go back to the idea that Matt and Kate could take you to court. What would you and Dalia do?"

"Well, I guess we'd have to hire a lawyer."

"What would happen if you hired a lawyer?"

"It would be very expensive. And if Matt and Kate won the case, we'd face bankruptcy because we can't afford the project on our own."

"What would happen then?"

"We'd move out of the fixer upper."

"And if you lost everything and had to find another place to live, what would happen then?"

Randy paused with a pained look on his face before replying, "Dalia and I would have to start all over again from the ground up."

"So you could find a smaller apartment that wasn't torn up, and your living situation would radically improve?"

Randy nodded.

"Would you still have your real estate license?"

He thought for a moment. "Yes. I could still work, but I might be too embarrassed to stay at the real estate agency I work for now."

"Would you look for another agency?"

"I suppose so. I could probably find another broker somewhere."

"Would Dalia still be able to work as an interior designer?"

"Yes."

I sat back for a moment to let him digest that possibility. "So if the worst-case scenario occurs in the business partnership—Matt and Kate quit, sue you, and you go bankrupt—then you and your wife would move to a small apartment that would be a much better living situation than you have now. You would find a new agency to work for and start over. Right?"

"Yes, that pretty much sums it up."

I asked the key question: "Can you survive that?"

"What a mess. That would be horrible."

"Yes, but could you survive it?"

Randy frowned at me. "Would Dalia and I still be alive after all of that? Yes, I suppose we would. But our marriage might be in trouble."

"What would you do if that happened?"

"We'd come to you for couple's counseling."

I smiled and took us in another direction. "Let's try a different line of thought. Rather than trying to make other people happy at your own expense, what would happen if you sat down with Matt and Kate and calmly told them how you and Dalia feel? What if you tried to figure out a solution together?"

Randy acknowledged that he hadn't done that. "It's really not fair for me to blame all of this on them. I don't think anyone is doing this to me on purpose. I suspect everyone feels disappointed in how long it's taken, and because of that, we all get defensive. I just wish I'd gotten to know them better before we got into this arrangement."

"So you blame yourself?"

"Somewhat," he admitted. "I want to take responsibility for my part."

"Any partnership can go sour. This happens between people who have known each other for years. I think the place to start is forgiving yourself for making this arrangement. You thought you made the best decision at the time."

"It seemed providential at the time—to meet a couple that had the same goal and compatible skills. It seemed perfect."

"It's okay to make mistakes and learn from them."

"Yes, I need to stop being so hard on myself. Maybe this situation can still be salvaged if we calmly talk it through."

"You've already faced the worst-case scenario no matter how this plays out. Either you let go of your resentment of Matt and Kate, allow Dalia to speak for herself, and move forward on fixing the house, or it all falls apart, and you end up with bankruptcy, a better place to live, and you continue your careers."

"I can survive this, can't I? I can get up the courage to talk with Dalia and come up with our own plan. Then we can talk with Matt and Kate. No matter what, Dalia and I will be okay."

"Yes, you can," I said. "You've got choices. You're much stronger than you realize. So is Dalia."

Step Five: Create a Courageous Brain

Randy had suffered trauma in his childhood. His mother mismanaged her anger and became abusive, while his father abandoned Randy when he needed protection. Abuse and abandonment are direct threats to our survival. The fear that Randy's childhood instilled in him is real, and to some degree, we all have to face this fear of being hurt again.

When we're hurt, we often experience anger. Anger is a victim's emotion, and Randy was genuinely victimized as a child. All of us are victimized to some extent in life, but if we take that identification into adulthood, we can see ourselves as victims (with a capital V). We give up our adult power and live as if we are perpetual children, abdicating control of our own lives.

When we see ourselves as victims, we also risk becoming offenders ourselves. When we are hurt, we may lash out at others as a way of avoiding the more vulnerable emotions: feeling hurt, rejected, blamed, or abandoned. All of the emotions we've covered in this book can hit us all at once. This creates a destructive cycle wherein two people are constantly hurting and being hurt. That's why we need to confront these emotions in a healthy way before they explode. When we do so, we define ourselves as the capable people we are at the present time.

To calm our brains and think clearly, we need to ask ourselves what we are most afraid of in this confrontation. Perhaps you are afraid that your anger will take control—that you'll say or do things you could regret. Perhaps you're afraid the other person will blow up. Maybe you're afraid of damaging or losing the relationship. But I assure you that by refusing to engage in honest communication, the relationship will be damaged.

We create a courageous brain by realizing we can handle what we are most afraid of. Once we have identified our greatest fear, we can ask ourselves if this fear is even likely to occur. Most of the time, catastrophizing thoughts warp the situation. They tell us the relationship will be ruined, or the person will never listen to us anyway. Those assumptions are rarely fair or accurate. But if the worst-case scenario did occur, we need to acknowledge that we would survive it. If the conversation triggers our past wounds, we can step away to calm ourselves. If we lose the relationship, we can handle the consequences.

As we recognize this, our brains will begin to calm down. When our brains are calm, we regain our ability to empathize with the other person. We can identify and discard any false assumptions we are projecting onto them. We also regain the ability to understand what's happening inside ourselves, and we have to understand ourselves before we can expect someone else to understand us. But above all else, we can be sure we will survive whatever outcome occurs.

Focused Meditation Exercise:

This fifteen-minute exercise is designed to help you face the fear of confrontation. The more you repeat this exercise, the more quickly your brain will be able to calm down when conflict arises. It will strengthen the part of your brain that thinks critically and empathizes to create win-win situations. Before you start, you'll want to find a comfortable place free of interruptions.

Escape the Fear Trap of Confrontation
Begin

After you find a comfortable place free of interruptions, take deep breaths through your nose and out your mouth. Scan your body from top to bottom, noting areas where you are holding stress.

You may feel tightness in your neck or shoulders or in your face and jaw. Breathe deeply into these areas and allow yourself to relax. You are safe and competent. There's no need to hold on to stress any longer.

Move down your body to your shoulders and arms, your hands and fingers. Release any tension you find there. Notice the depth of your breath. Is it shallow and quick or deep and slow? Take time to slow down your breathing, and take deeper and deeper breaths until you see your abdomen rising and not your shoulders.

Focus on your midsection. Are you holding stress inside yourself? Do you feel any pain? Focus attention on the back of your body. Is there stress between your shoulder blades? Breathe deeply and allow these muscles to relax. Move down to your middle and lower back. Again, imagine breathing into those muscles and release all tension.

Move to your pelvic area and buttocks. Are you holding tension in those large muscles? Allow your breath to fill up your core to relieve stress and replace it with a sense of competency and personal power.

Move down your thighs, knees, and calves, first focusing on your right leg and then your left leg. Rotate your feet and wiggle your toes to allow the stress to pour out of your body and into the floor.

5-Minute Mark

Today we will focus on grounding you in self-confidence, compassion, and courage. Think about the person you want to talk with about an unresolved issue. We often start at a place of anxiety and imagine the worst that could happen in this type of conversation. Instead, think about the best attributes this person possesses. Find specific things about this person that you respect and enjoy. If this is a particularly toxic relationship, there might be only one or two traits that you respect. Be authentic in the characteristics that you choose.

From this restful place, ask yourself the question, "What do I like about this person?"

You might answer, "I like her work ethic," or "I like how he's always optimistic." For the next several minutes, repeat this affirmation to yourself.

- On the inhale, ask, "What do I like about this person?"
- On the exhale, say, "I like [fill in the blank]." Allow yourself to feel positive about this person.
- Inhale: "What do I like about this person?"
- Exhale: "I like [fill in the blank]."

Concentrate on this positive trait as you become more and more convinced this is true. If you notice your mind shifting to the things you don't like about this person, gently bring your attention back to the positive. Allow yourself to have empathy for them and assume the best about them.

8-Minute Mark

It's time to focus on taking responsibility for your own side of the relationship. You are in charge of understanding yourself and then helping others understand your thoughts and feelings. If you don't tell them how you feel or what you need, others can't respond. It's not up to them to guess or read your mind.

- On the inhale, ask, "What do I want or need from this person?"
- On the exhale, answer, "I want or need [fill in the blank]."

Repeat this process and notice that you become more confident with each breath. Repeat this exercise with additional things you need or want from this person. Allow yourself to believe that this person is able to respond positively to your request.

11-Minute Mark

Imagine that you are talking to this person and letting them know what you want or need from them or the situation. Continue to breathe deeply, especially if your mind focuses on the worst-case scenario. Remind yourself that you can take care of yourself, no matter how this person responds.

- On the inhale, affirm to yourself, "I will do my best."
- On the exhale, state, "I am safe and secure no matter the outcome."

Repeat this affirmation while noticing your breath. Has your breathing become shallow, or has it remained deep? As you repeat the affirmation, allow your mind to scan your body and note any places of tension. Allow this affirmation to speak to those areas of stress and bring relaxation and confidence to your entire body.

14-Minute Mark

Slowly bring yourself back to the outside world. Take a few more deep breaths.

15-Minute Mark

How do you feel about yourself and the other person after this meditation? If you repeat this exercise on a regular basis, your sense of confidence to handle conflict will increase. You will also find it easier to talk calmly about your feelings, needs, and concerns.

When you feel less anxious about having to confront an uncomfortable situation, you will be more equipped to stay true to your feelings, express them with less anger or defensiveness, and be able to cope regardless of the outcome. New pathways will be formed, and it will be easier to assume good faith about the other person. If they do not respond as you hope, you can be confident in your own strength and integrity.

Step Six: Live Free of the Fear Trap

Randy and I worked in preparation for the meeting he knew he could no longer avoid. Tension was mounting in the group, and one day he said, "Today's the day. It's time for the talk."

Randy was smiling the next time he came into my office. He said down and declared, "Well, that went better than I expected and a little worse than I'd hoped."

Randy and Dalia came home after work and, as usual, found Matt and Kate still working in the house. Randy asked if they could all sit down together for a moment. At first, Matt resisted, saying that he had a lot of work yet to do before they could go home. "I asked again, saying it was important, and the four of us sat down around the kitchen table, which was covered with dust, I might add.

"I started out by saying that we all went into this project in good faith and with high hopes. We've all done our best, and yet it's taken much longer than we expected. Matt interrupted me to defend himself, and I asked him to let me finish what I was saying. I assured him that I wasn't angry or wanting to blame anyone, and, to my surprise, that's exactly how I felt. I wanted to find a solution.

"I said that since the time table hasn't been achieved, a new arrangement needs to be made. Kate asked, 'So what does that mean for us? You are changing the agreement without our input.' I said that the plan was changed when, with our combined best efforts, the deadline was missed. It's been quite a long time now. Because of that, yes, the arrangement needs to be renegotiated.

"Matt leaned back and said nothing. I continued. 'Dalia and I need to find a different place to live until the project is completed. That means that we'll have less to contribute to the remodel.' Matt and Kate looked at each other, none too happy about that.

"I persisted. 'We are all investing much more time and money than expected.'

"Matt huffed, 'That's for sure.'

"'Then, Matt, I think that gives us at least three options. One, we stay in this partnership but review the budget and revise the entire plan. Two, one of us buys out the other, and we go our separate ways. And, three, we sell the house as is right now, pay off what we owe, and if there's any profit left over, we split it fifty-fifty.'

"Kate had tears in her eyes but nodded. She reached over to Dalia, and they hugged. 'I'm sorry it's turning out this way,' Kate said, and Dalia nodded.

"Matt said, 'Well, Kate and I need time to think about this. I don't like the fact that you're pushing this onto us. We're not the bad guys.' Before I could say anything else, he got up and stormed out of the room. Kate looked embarrassed and followed him out. They stopped coming to the house to work, but we have a meeting set up for this weekend to hammer out the details."

"How are you feeling?"

Randy sighed. "I'm so relieved. I feel like a huge weight is off my shoulders, and Dalia is so proud of me." He winked. "She has been very clear in showing her newfound respect for her strong husband."

We both laughed. "Do you feel like you've forgiven yourself for avoiding this problem?"

"Yes, and I'm not harboring the same resentment toward Matt and Kate. It's like I've forgiven everyone. Now all I want to do is come to some arrangement and get on with our lives."

Randy learned that it's easy to be resentful when we're not taking care of business. The primitive part of our brain wants us to hold on to our grudges because it wants to make sure we never find ourselves in a similar situation again. When we fret and stew, our brain produces dopamine, which plays a role in feeling pleasure. Our fear center rewards us for worrying, as if worrying, by itself, will keep us safe. In actuality, we are safe when we take proper actions to protect ourselves.

The challenge for Randy was to recognize that worrying, in itself, is not a solution. Instead, we must accept the reality of the situation. Whatever happened has happened. We can't change the past. It's already over. But we can change the future by changing the way we view and respond to the situation.

Like Randy, most of us believe we see the world in an objective way. We believe what we see is the way things really are. However, the version of reality we see is often distorted by our perceptual biases. Our biases reflect our wounds and the age we were when we sustained them. As noted before, we can respond from various emotional ages, regardless of our actual chronological age.

Steps to Forgiveness

First, we all have the need to be understood, especially when we are in pain. Find someone who will listen to you and give you room to experience your feelings. Some people will try to talk you out of your anger or resentment, which will not help you. You need to have a safe place where you can describe your experience and express your emotions. When we are validated, it helps us take the next step.

Second, we must accept the fact that a difficult thing occurred, and we cannot change the outcome. Many of us are reluctant to accept how horribly we've been hurt. It's far more difficult to accept it if our offender was a loved one or if we felt weak or ashamed. That's natural. We long for a happier ending or outcome—a rosier twist so we don't have to deal with the pain of reality. It may take some time before you're willing to acknowledge that nothing can change what happened. It has already occurred. It's critical to accept what happened and that the experience was hurtful to you.

The third step is to realize that what the other person did had nothing to do with you. Their behavior solely reflected who they were at the time. Something you said or did may have triggered their intense actions, but you did not "cause" or "force" the other person to be cruel, abusive, or insensitive.

Taking a step back from the situation will allow you to simply observe the other person's behavior. Don't take responsibility for anything they did or said. The person who hurt you was immersed in their own internal wounds, unable or unwilling to take your feelings into account. When we can calm our own feelings to realize this, it's easier to release any blame you might feel for what they did or said.

In the fourth step, it's important to see that your actions are your responsibility and yours alone. If you acted poorly, the other person is not to blame—just as you are not to blame for their actions. It can be challenging to see beyond our own biases to take ownership of what we did wrong. But we all have weaknesses, and it's in our best interest to acknowledge them.

When we are triggered, we are not rational. We can be blinded by the baggage from our past. When we allow ourselves to feel our fears without trying to ignore or bury them, we can see the humanity in ourselves and others. We are good and bad, weak and strong, perfect and imperfect. Accepting this allows us to feel compassion, which opens the door for forgiveness.

We must step back and recognize that we have biases just like everyone else. We do not see the world objectively. Most people hurt others out of their own wounded places. Often, a person will act out against someone else because of something they're struggling with inside themselves rather than anything the other person did. When we realize this, we can let the pain and resentment go.

It's important to forgive yourself and others for what has happened in the past. It's the best gift of healing you can give yourself. When we forgive, feelings of anger, hatred, and oppression are lifted. You can free yourself of those negative feelings that sit heavily in your chest, twist knots in your belly, and spin through your head.

Forgiveness does not mean the hurt you experienced was okay. In fact, forgiveness is an acknowledgment that the hurt did indeed occur and that you suffered from it. It's important for you to hold the offender accountable for their actions. The person who hurt you may never ask for forgiveness. The choice to forgive is primarily for your benefit, not theirs. It can release you from the emotions that tie you to this person in a harmful way. Forgiveness relinquishes the power the offender had over you. It is a statement that you will no longer allow yourself to be defined by this abuse. You declare yourself a survivor and a thriver; someone who has overcome the difficult experiences of the past.

You can forgive because this process allows you to build new neuropathways. You can literally go around the pathway of hurt recorded in your brain. It's not some vaporous, positive-thinking magic that disappears as soon as you stop thinking a positive thought. No, it's a real solution that becomes part of your actual body. It's a real solution that stays with you for the rest of your life.

Mayo Clinic has reported that the health benefits of forgiveness include lower blood pressure, less stress, fewer symptoms of depression, stronger immune system, and improved heart health. Forgiveness, when done right, is freeing.

When we forgive, we are no longer driven by the desire for revenge. Randy needed to move past resentment to the freedom of forgiveness. I define forgiveness as choosing to release yourself from the anger you hold against someone who hurt you or even against yourself. Forgiveness helps you create better relationships with others and with yourself. You may not want to continue a relationship with someone who hurt you, but if the other person takes responsibility for what he or she has done, the relationship may be salvageable. This is up to you.

Key Points

- As children, we needed adults to protect us and treat us with respect.
- We also needed adult role models to show us how to deal with conflict and anger management.

- Without proper role models, we can grow into adulthood without knowing how to properly navigate conflict in a way that is constructive rather than destructive.
- If we don't know how to deal with conflict, we become afraid of it. When we're in the fear trap of confrontation, our ways of coping with conflict are extremely limited (fight, flee, or freeze).
- We may try to avoid conflict by stifling our anger or trying to please others.
- This often results in passive-aggressive behaviors, where we stifle our anger but release it in subtle forms that annoy or upset others.
- We may also hold in the anger until we explode and say or do things that are hurtful to others.
- We may blame the other person for our feelings and overlook how we played a role in the conflict.
- Effective confrontation is simply telling others how we feel and finding a win-win solution.
- When we escape the fear trap of confrontation, we have numerous options for resolution. Our frontal lobe—the center of empathy and problem solving—is activated, allowing us to see from the other person's point of view.
- We often realize the other party didn't have a malicious motive toward us. It is their issue, even if it is directed at us. When we realize this, we develop compassion toward ourselves and others.
- If others refuse to admit they hurt us, we can choose to discontinue the relationship with them. We can still forgive them to release ourselves from the negative emotions that tie us to them and hold us in anger.
- Forgiveness is the process by which we free ourselves from the fear trap of confrontation.

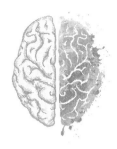

Are You Afraid of Being Ignored?

People are like stained-glass windows. They sparkle and shine
when the sun is out, but when the darkness sets in, their true
beauty is revealed only if there is a light from within.
—*Elisabeth Kübler-Ross*

I had to hold the phone away from my ear as Aya screamed. "I have to see you! You'll never believe what my husband did!" Fearing he had committed a criminal act, I agreed to meet with them that same day.

I'd been working with this young couple in their early thirties for about a year and a half when they hit an impasse in their relationship. This was Aya's second marriage but Jeff's first. They met when Jeff brought his beloved bulldog, Lilly, into the pet store that Aya managed. Their shared love for the breed soon blossomed into romance and a wedding, which included Lilly as the "flower dog."

I greeted them in the waiting room. In spite of their common interest in bulldogs, Aya and Jeff looked as mismatched as a Great Dane and a Chihuahua. Aya, a Japanese American, was five feet tall and barely weighed one hundred pounds. Perfectly groomed, she had a special way of putting colors together, and she always looked polished and attractive. She made quite a statement when she entered a room, though at the moment she seemed to have been swallowed up by the waiting-room chair.

Jeff, in contrast, was a tall Swede with red-blonde hair and a large, stocky frame. Barely squeezing into his chair, he sported a well-worn green fleece, jeans, and a wool hat. I suspected Jeff, a fairly popular local artist, had been interrupted mid–painting project to attend the session—he was unshaven with short stubble, and his unwashed hands were stained a rainbow of colors. When they stood up, he towered over Aya by what looked like a foot and a half. I invited them into my office.

Step One: Tell Your Story

I'd barely shut the door when Aya launched into her story. "Okay, about three months ago, Jeff started making his own peanut butter from raw peanuts."

"It's really good peanut butter," Jeff interjected.

Aya concurred. "Yes, it is, actually. I'm really glad Jeff is interested in healthier eating, but here's the part about Lilly. I love animals. I see them at work all day long, but I don't want them in my kitchen. It's an oasis for me. I love to cook, and I don't want to deal with a dog in my kitchen."

"Our kitchen," Jeff corrected her.

Aya continued, undeterred. "Jeff agreed Lilly could go anywhere but the kitchen. But yesterday, I came home from work early, and what did I find in my kitchen?"

"Our kitchen," Jeff corrected her again.

This time she glared at him while he sat back a bit. Looking at me, she said as calmly as she could, "Not only did I walk in to see Lilly in the kitchen—which was bad enough—but Jeff had fed her some of his peanut butter, and he was scraping her leftover peanut butter out of her bowl and into my jar."

"Your jar?"

"Well, let's call it the 'people jar,' okay?" she shot back. "It's the jar that you and I share, which does not include Lilly."

While they bickered, I realized I had a stunned look on my face when Aya looked back at me and smiled. Jeff looked annoyed and a bit befuddled. I asked Jeff to tell his point of view.

"Well, eating leftover peanut butter from Lilly's bowl has never hurt us. It wasn't a problem for Aya until she found out about it. What's the big deal?"

"What's the big deal? First of all, you agreed to keep Lilly out of the kitchen. You know how to handle dogs. Second, I've been eating peanut butter contaminated by dog saliva. Third, you purposely didn't tell me because you knew I'd be upset. I feel like you completely ignore my feelings." She started to cry. "I think you love Lilly more than you love me. In fact, I don't believe you love me anymore. If you don't apologize to me right now, I may just file for divorce!"

Jeff rolled his eyes.

She huffed. "Don't dismiss me, Jeff. I'm so angry. I don't know how much longer I can do this with you."

He shook his head. "I don't know either. Aya, I'm so tired of this drama over things that don't matter."

Step Two: Identify Your Triggers

I asked Aya to see me without Jeff, and we made an appointment for the next day. Aya and I dove into her feelings more deeply. From my past work with her, I already knew that Aya grew up in a middle-class suburb of Cincinnati. Her mother was born in America to Japanese immigrants, and her father emigrated from Japan in the mid-1980s. Both parents were well-respected professionals. Her mother, Sumiyo, was a physician's assistant, and her father, Sanji, worked as a liaison at a Japanese bank with a large branch in Cincinnati. Aya was their only child.

When Aya was around eight, she and her parents went on a family vacation to a cabin on a lake. Aya hadn't learned how to swim, and she was eager for her dad to teach her. There was a pier that led from the land into the lake. Aya and her father walked to the end of the landing and looked across the water.

"Aya, let's jump in here, and I'll teach you how to swim," her dad said.

Aya shook her head no. "Let's go to the shore. I don't want to jump in here. It's too deep."

Her dad insisted that the water was shallow enough for her and kept coaxing her to jump. "Come on, Aya! It will be fun." But the more he pressured her to jump, the more resistant she became.

"No, I don't want to go into that lake!" she yelled.

As she turned to leave the landing, her father grabbed her by the waist and hoisted her into the water. Aya panicked and began to thrash. Her dad laughed. "You're fine, Aya. Just stand up. The water isn't deep enough for you to drown."

But Aya was so disoriented when she went under that she didn't know which way was up. She swallowed a great deal of water while submerged. Finally, Sanji realized she was in real danger of drowning, so he jumped in and pulled her to safety. Aya's mother heard the commotion from the cabin and came out to find her daughter spitting up water and crying loudly. She ran to Aya's side.

"What happened, Sanji?" she cried out.

Sanji shook his head in remorse. "I didn't mean to hurt her."

"You threw her into the lake?" Sumiyo screeched with astonishment.

"Yes. She was being overly dramatic. I thought she'd stand up and find the whole thing funny."

"Funny?" her mother demanded. "How is this funny?"

"I'm really sorry. I'd never do anything to hurt her—you know that."

"Come on, Aya," her mom said. "Let's get you inside."

Shortly after they returned to the cabin, Aya started vomiting. The lake water wasn't clean, and she became very ill. Since her mother was a physician's assistant, she quickly treated her daughter for infections from the lake water bacteria she'd ingested. Her father apologized profusely. But due to this experience, Aya became very fearful of two things: being near water and catching diseases. She never tried to swim again and often fussed about germs and cleanliness.

When Aya was in the ninth grade, there was an outbreak of lice at her high school. In her homeroom, five of her twenty classmates had the pesky bugs roaming on top of their heads. Aya became afraid of catching lice.

She never "caught the bug," but this started a cycle of excessive cleanliness due to the fear of contracting an unexpected illness.

During the lice outbreak, she felt that her parents had dismissed her fears. She wanted to wash her hair every night and kept asking her mother to check her scalp for nits. At first, they thought she was just being conscientious, but after weeks, both her parents became frustrated with her obsession. At dinner one night, her dad reached his limit. He slammed his fist on the table and hollered, "I don't want to hear any more about this!" Aya looked at her mother for support, but her mom looked down. Aya was banned from mentioning her anxiety again.

"I always knew my father was truly sorry about throwing me into the lake, so I forgave him. But when they refused to talk about my fears over the lice, my relationship with my parents changed radically. Before 'the ban,' as I call it, I felt like my parents understood and loved me. But when they refused to even listen to the history of my fears, I felt totally dismissed. My feelings were unimportant to them—just a horrible intrusion into their lives. So I became invisible. The sense of betrayal was enormous, especially toward my mother, in whom I had always confided.

"I realize my disgust isn't simply about Lilly and the peanut butter," Aya shuddered. "But that part is really disgusting."

How Many Thoughts Do You Have Each Day?

Negative self-talk is one way that we strengthen negative neuropathways in our brains. Some research suggests that we have an average of sixty thousand to eighty thousand thoughts per day. If a majority of these thoughts are negative—about ourselves, other people, or life in general—the potential for triggering our brain's stress hormones is staggeringly high.

In fact, you are in control of your thoughts if you decide to change the chemical pathways in your brain. While it's important for you to identify your emotions rather than repress them, you do not need to be victimized by them. You have the power to see feelings as they are and set yourself free.

I grinned. "I tend to agree with you. We need to address this in our next couple's session."

Aya agreed. "It's more about how Jeff disregards my feelings. I feel unheard—like Jeff doesn't care about me or my happiness. And I've been hurt in the past by people not listening to me when I say I'm scared or don't want something to happen."

Aya's First Trigger: Her Clear Request Being Violated

Death may be humanity's greatest fear, but dealing with our mortality is something we must all face. Even though Aya was not in mortal danger, she reacted to the peanut butter episode as if she might die. Because of her near-drowning experience as a child, she couldn't properly distinguish between a true threat to her life and a trigger that reminded her of genuine danger.

None of us like being ignored. We all want our needs to be acknowledged and our boundaries to be honored. But Aya associated this violation of her specific requests with mortal danger. Her amygdala was triggered, and she could no longer think reasonably about the situation.

When Aya found Lilly in the kitchen, she realized Jeff had violated their agreement. As she suspected, he had been letting the dog into the kitchen on a regular basis. Aya was flooded with anxiety. That was upsetting, but when Aya discovered that she had been eating peanut butter contaminated with dog slobber, she fell deep into a fear trap.

When we have proper boundaries in place, no other human being can pose a danger to us.

Suddenly she felt like her younger self, who suffered from her father's poor judgment. On one hand, most of us would not want to eat peanut butter taken from a dog dish. Being upset may have been appropriate, but because Aya was triggered, her reaction was extreme.

She overreacted by acting as if her life was threatened, and that she couldn't rely on Jeff anymore. She equated his lack of concern for sanitation as a lack of concern for her. Aya decided Jeff's behavior could mean only one thing: he no longer loved her, and their marriage was about to end.

When we have proper boundaries in place, no other human being can pose a danger to us. You could stand two feet from a serial killer completely unharmed if there was a thick glass wall between you. Boundaries, physical or relational, are meant to protect us from undue vulnerability and possible danger.

Aya had set her boundaries with Jeff, but he violated them. As far as Jeff was concerned, these boundaries were inconsequential. To Aya, violating the boundaries was a matter of life and death. She summed up her feelings like this: "Seeing Jeff contaminate our food was the same way I felt when my father threw me in the water and later refused to hear my fears. I may be overreacting, but it's how I see this situation. He won't protect me if he doesn't think my fears are warranted. I feel like he doesn't love me."

Aya's Second Trigger: Jeff's Refusal to Take Responsibility for His Choices

A second trigger was Jeff shrugging off their agreements. He didn't apologize for breaking his promise about keeping Lilly out of the kitchen. He dismissed Anya's objections to feeding her the peanut butter and putting the uneaten portion back into their jar. When Jeff wouldn't admit he'd violated her boundaries, he instead mocked her anxiety.

Aya felt doubly violated. First, he broke his promise, and, in her mind, put her in danger; second, he refused to see he had done anything wrong. He didn't listen to her when she set her boundaries, and he didn't listen again when she told him how upset she was.

Step Three: Describe Patterns of Self-Sabotage

An important part of Aya's healing was to understand that how we talk to ourselves impacts how we feel. While there are a number of self-destructive thought patterns, here are four that can be seen in Aya's response to fear:

Demoralizing or discouraging self-talk: "I am a fool to think anyone will love me or listen to me."

Automatic counterproductive thoughts when triggered: "Jeff does not care about how I feel. He loves that dog more than he loves me."

Irrational and highly limiting beliefs: "I will only be happy if Jeff hears me and does what I want."

Catastrophizing thoughts of obsessive worry over an unlikely outcome: "My marriage will be doomed if Jeff lets that dog back into the kitchen."

We have long outgrown the strategies developed at the age of two or seven or fourteen. Unfortunately, the more we repeat these outdated patterns, the more ingrained they become in our brains.

As we've discussed, we did our best to protect ourselves when we were first wounded by events from our childhood. As children, our options were limited because we were dependent on our parents and caregivers to meet our basic needs. Our brains were not fully developed, so we were unable to create realistic solutions to the threats in our lives. Depending on our age, we may have cried, thrown tantrums, mistreated a younger sibling, or even tried to run away. But since we were unable to drive away or pay our own rent, we were ultimately stuck in the situation, having to cope the best we could.

Once we learn a response that "works," we continue it. However, coping responses in childhood are immature and ineffective in adulthood. We have long outgrown the strategies developed at the age of two or seven or fourteen. Unfortunately, the more we repeat these outdated patterns, the more ingrained they become in our brains.

I'd like to congratulate you because whatever you did to survive worked—as proven by the fact that you are still alive and reading this book. But you are an adult now, no longer dependent on your parents or caregivers the way you were as a child. It's time to see that your childhood defenses are now setting you up for failure.

Self-Sabotage Pattern One: Assuming What Others Think Without Asking Them

Aya fumed. "Why am I so naïve? Jeff won't keep agreements or even be a decent human being. He doesn't seem to understand hygiene or diseases or anything."

"Did you ask him how he feels about you?"

"No. I don't need to ask. He doesn't love me anymore. He doesn't care if I'm frightened or upset."

Aya said a variety of negative things about herself and Jeff, such as:

"I'm a fool to have trusted him to be hygienic."

"Jeff doesn't listen to me, just like my parents."

"He loves that slobbery dog more than he loves me."

"I'm ready to kick him and his dirty dog out of the house."

Are You Missing Cues from Your Body?

The cause behind anxiety or depression can seem mysterious, but sometimes we miss the clues in our bodies. Oftentimes, we can find an explanation with a closer look at how our brain is operating.

For example, research has shown that people who felt neglected or unheard as children often have irregular levels of cortisol (primary stress hormone). Irregular cortisol levels often contribute to psychological disorders like anxiety, depression, and PTSD.

This irregularity also hinders our ability to regulate our own emotions. The good news is that we can change our hormone levels. When we become aware of their role in our bodies, we can seek more well-rounded solutions to our mental health issues.

The cause behind anxiety or depression can seem mysterious, but sometimes we miss the clues in our bodies. Oftentimes, we can find an explanation with a closer look at how our brain is operating.

For example, research has shown that people who felt neglected or unheard as children often have irregular levels of cortisol (primary stress hormone). Irregular cortisol levels often contribute to psychological disorders like anxiety, depression, and PTSD.

This irregularity also hinders our ability to regulate our own emotions. The good news is that we can change our hormone levels. When we become aware of their role in our bodies, we can seek more well-rounded solutions to our mental health issues.

"Aya, you are assuming the worst about Jeff, and in reality, you don't know how he feels. Unless you talk with someone, you can only guess at how the other person feels. Assumptions can be dangerous to a relationship. Only Jeff can tell us how he feels. I think we need to focus on you right now and not assume that you know what's going on with him."

The truth was that Aya didn't know what Jeff was thinking or feeling. They talked past each other, neither of them listening. Once she was convinced he didn't love her, she threatened to end the marriage. Her amygdala was in control, and all she knew to do was to fight, flee, or freeze. She wanted to run away.

Self-Sabotage Pattern Two: Giving Away Personal Power

In spite of the massive amount of drama that occurred over the peanut butter issue, the problem could have been easily solved. Aya could simply have her own jar of homemade peanut butter and never eat out of Jeff's jar at all. She'd never have to worry about eating dog-contaminated peanut butter again.

Unless you talk with someone, you can only guess at how the other person feels. Assumptions can be dangerous to a relationship.

But Aya wouldn't entertain this solution. She had given so much of her personal power over to Jeff that she wasn't creative about a solution. When Jeff violated her boundaries (and then some), she was triggered and became an eight-year-old girl again. Adult women have more power than eight-year-old girls in enforcing their boundaries.

Eight-year-old girls are physically smaller and less emotionally mature. Even though Aya, as an adult, was capable of enforcing her boundaries, she played the victim and threatened that she'd leave if Jeff did not do what she said.

People using threats are stuck in a fear trap. In cases of domestic violence, leaving an abusive marriage is often the solution. But Aya was not in that situation, even if she felt like it in the moment. Aya had no confidence in herself to enforce her boundaries with Jeff, which was the underlying reason she felt so powerless. She began to believe the only way she could be safe was to get away from her husband and his dog.

Step Four: Imagine the Worst-Case Scenario

I asked her to tell me specifically what she was afraid would happen to her.

Aya didn't hesitate. "Well, for starters, I could have gotten sick."

"Is Lilly sick?"

"No, but I still could have gotten sick."

"What happened when you got sick at the lake?"

"My mother took care of me. I threw up a lot, sort of like food poisoning, and I got well in a few days."

"What would have happened if you got sick from the dog?"

She was irate. "I could have died!"

I smiled at her. "What are the chances you would have died from a disease from Lilly?"

Aya frowned. "It could have happened."

"But if you did get sick, what would have happened?"

"Jeff would have gotten me to the ER, and I'd have been treated."

I nodded. "And then?"

"I'd get well, but I would be all the angrier with Jeff for breaking his promise and getting me sick."

"So if you got angry with Jeff and blamed him for your illness, what would happen after that?"

She turned her nose up in the air. "I'd tell him it was me or Lilly."

"You love Lilly almost as much as Jeff does."

"Yes, but this is different. He can't indulge her and ignore me."

"So if you made him choose between you and Lilly, what would happen?"

Aya frowned. "I honestly don't know. If I made him choose between us, I think he might choose her. He'd be so upset if I drew that line in the sand."

"Let's say he chose you. What then?"

"I'd be upset because I don't want to give Lilly away."

"So it's not about the dog, is it?"

"No, I don't want to live without either of them."

"If you were thinking about getting a divorce, what would you do?"

"We'd come here and talk to you, hoping to find a solution."

I sat back. "Aya, if the worst-case scenario occurred, you'd be right where you are today. You are essentially living out your worst-case scenario. Can you survive today?"

"Yes, I can."

"The worst thing you can think of happening is that you'd get into marriage counseling and find a way through this difficult time. The two of you have to find a way to set and honor each other's boundaries. Hopefully, you can."

Step Five: Create a Courageous Brain

When someone's actions or words trigger us, it's the child in us that responds. In Aya's case, Jeff's actions caused her inner eight year old to panic. As an eight year old, she could not protect herself from being thrown in the lake. She needed an adult to protect her boundaries. As a grown woman, she acted as if she still needed an adult to come reinforce her boundaries. She gave up her personal power over the situation. Her fear blinded her from seeing that she was now the adult she needed.

We experience fear when we are triggered. There is no shame in experiencing this fear. But we need to realize that we are the accumulation of all of the years we have lived. When we need self-comforting, we are the competent adult who can be the source of nurturance. When you need protection, we are the strong adult who can protect. This way, we both validate our feelings and soothe our own fears.

Focused Meditation Exercise:

When you feel your needs are not being met, this fourteen-minute exercise reminds you of your own strength and capability. Over time, you will be able to regain your sense of safety, set boundaries to protect your needs, and communicate what you need from those around you.

Escape the Fear Trap of Being Ignored
Begin

Get into a comfortable position with your arms and legs uncrossed. Breathe in through your nose and exhale through your mouth. You may be breathing shallowly, primarily from your chest. Focus your attention on breathing deeply into your abdomen. It may take a while to relax to the point where your stomach expands and retracts with each slow breath. Continue to breathe in through your nose and out through your mouth.

5-Minute Mark

Now that you are more relaxed, imagine yourself, as an adult, sitting in a room with yourself as a child. As this picture comes into your mind, notice what age you are. What are you wearing? What are you feeling?

- As you breathe in, say to the child-self, "You are safe because…"
- On the exhale, say, "I am here with you."
- Repeat this as many times as you choose.
- On the inhale, say, "You are safe because…"
- On the exhale, say, "I protect you."

Repeat this as many times as you choose.

- On the next inhale, say, "You are safe because…"
- On the exhale, say, "I pay attention to your needs."
- Repeat this as many times as you choose.

- On the inhale, say, "You are safe because…"
- On the exhale, say whatever affirmation comes to your mind.

Repeat this as many times as you choose.

For the next few minutes, repeat these assurances or create your own that meet the specific needs of who you were as a child.

As an adult, you can protect your child-self. Allow yourself to feel safe and protected.

10-Minute Mark

Imagine you are in the present moment, and you are talking kindly to yourself. We are replacing the negative self-talk with new affirmations.

- On the inhale, say, "My needs are important because…"
- On the exhale, say, "I am a person of value."
- Repeat this as many times as you choose.
- On the inhale, say, "I make my needs known because…"
- On the exhale, say, "I am an adult who speaks up."

Repeat this as many times as you choose.

- On the inhale, say, "I am safe because…"
- On the exhale, say, "I set boundaries that protect me."
- Repeat this as many times as you choose.

Continue this pattern by filling in the phrases that will strengthen your sense of safety. You are not invisible. You are an important person who deserves to be safe and have your needs met.

14-Minute Mark

It's time to bring your attention to the present moment. Your inner world has been changed through this meditation. Your brain has been soothed. The fear center of your brain has been deactivated, and new neuropathways have been formed. You will strengthen these pathways every time you do this focused meditation.

As you continue this, you will be more able to soothe yourself when you feel invisible or like no one understands you. The more you pay attention to yourself and the more you understand yourself, the more you will be able to share with others what you need. The more you love yourself, the more you will believe in your own worth and value.

Now wiggle your fingers and toes and slowly bring yourself back to the outside world.

Take a few more deep breaths. You are now ready to engage with your life, newly energized to be confident and able to speak up for yourself.

Step Six: Live Free of the Fear Trap

Aya and I met for a month, and she meditated daily in between sessions. Her sense of self-worth grew; she felt more confident and less threatened. She asked if Jeff could join her in our next session, and I agreed that would be a positive step.

Jeff and Aya sat in my office with a renewed hope for their relationship. Jeff looked at me and said, "I love her. I just haven't understood why she gets so upset over things that don't matter at all to me."

I felt compassion for Jeff and responded, "I believe you. I don't think you have listened to the fear behind her words. Are you willing to see things from her perspective?"

"I'm willing to try."

"Without realizing it, Aya, you have also been oblivious to how Jeff feels."

Aya looked surprised for a moment, and then her face softened. "I can see that now. I've been upset that he hasn't been listening to me, but I've not listened to him either."

Aya looked over at Jeff. "I want to find a way to make it through this together."

"Neither of you have been listening to the other well, and that will have to change if you are going to be successful at this relationship. Aya, would you tell Jeff how it feels when he doesn't honor your boundaries?"

"Jeff, I feel very frightened because of what happened in my past. I'm working on catching myself before I overreact, but I need you to keep our agreements. That's basic kindness and respect."

Jeff nodded his head in agreement. "I honestly didn't think having Lilly in the kitchen was such a big deal for you, and I'm sorry. I haven't been honest with you, and I've resented your rules. But I think we can renegotiate around Lilly so we're both comfortable."

"And what will you both do about the peanut butter?"

Aya wrinkled her nose. "I'm setting aside *my own jar*, and Jeff can eat all the dog slobber he wants. I don't ever want to go through that again."

Aya, as well as Jeff, learned that overcoming irrational fear can require stepping into a completely different paradigm. Aya took it upon herself to get her own peanut butter, setting a boundary with Jeff. She no longer felt the need to overdramatize the situation in order to get Jeff to act as she wanted. Jeff also changed his behavior, and this allowed trust to strengthen between them. Rather than pushing away people we love or even ending a relationship, we need to set proper boundaries that will protect us. We can protect ourselves, not by isolating ourselves but by setting clear rules about how we will allow ourselves to be treated.

Key Points

- As children, we need adults to keep us safe. If we were not properly protected or if someone violated our boundaries, we may have a core wound related to feeling unsafe.
- We also needed adult role models to show us how to communicate our needs and set clear emotional and physical boundaries to make sure they are addressed.
- Without proper role models, we can grow into adulthood without knowing how to set boundaries and make sure our needs are acknowledged and met.
- As adults, it is our responsibility to keep ourselves safe by setting proper boundaries. People who belong in our lives honor our boundaries. Some require stronger boundaries because they can harm us, either intentionally or unintentionally.
- It is our responsibility to set and enforce our boundaries. To keep ourselves safe, we must establish consequences that will occur if another person violates our boundaries.
- When we tell others that we feel afraid or uneasy, we must insist they honor our boundaries by listening and responding to us.

- If we are triggered, we may feel as if we are in serious danger when, in reality, we are not. This is an example of overreacting.
- As adults, we can comfort our own fears of not being safe or heard by understanding and protecting our own needs.

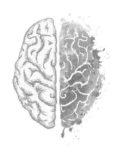

FEAR TRAP FIVE

Are You Afraid of Failure?

We can choose to be perfect and admired or to be real and loved.
—*Glennon Doyle Melton*

A handsome African-American man walked into my office. Flashing me a wide smile, he sat down on the couch with a sense of confidence and charm. He wore khaki pants and a crisp button-down shirt. He exuded an aura of success and looked as if he had every reason to be happy with his life.

I realized I'd seen Grant somewhere before. I asked him if we knew each other from another context.

"I don't think so, but you might have seen my picture in the paper recently. I took the lead on a case defending a large corporation in town against a lawsuit."

"Yes, I remember that article. It's been a long case, hasn't it?"

Grant smiled as he gazed at the trees outside through the window. "Winning that case has been the highlight of my career, and it doesn't hurt my chances for eventually running for political office."

"So you're interested in politics?"

"Yes. At least that's what my father has planned for me. He's the district attorney, and he always wanted to become a state senator. He ran but didn't win. So he's decided that I'll carry the family name into the capital. I just turned forty in February, and everything is falling into place regarding my career. But that's not why I'm here."

Step One: Tell Your Story

I asked Grant to tell me more. A flash of anger narrowed his eyes for just a second and then disappeared. As he began to talk, a slight smile took its place.

"Let's be clear about one thing: it's not my idea to be here. My wife wants to leave me, and she says if I don't see a professional, that's the last straw. Renee has been asking me to go to marriage counseling for a while now. I put her off, saying I was too busy on this case. But, of course, I have one case after another, so there has never been a good time. The truth is I didn't ever want to sit in an office like yours. No offense, of course."

"None taken," I said. "What made you resist going to counseling?"

He sort of glared at me as he replied. "It would mean that I failed in some way. I don't fail."

I took that in. The discrepancy between what he said and how he said it was a bit shocking—sad and angry words delivered with a smile and warmth. "And now?"

"She told me last week that she was finished. She wants a divorce, and she asked me to move out so she and the children could live there without disrupting their schooling. I was absolutely stunned. I said, 'What are you talking about? This is so sudden.'

"Renee looked at me and shook her head. She said she's been unhappy for years, and nothing she has done would get my attention. After I refused to go to marriage counseling with her, she got her own therapist. According to her, I've left her no choice but to end our marriage."

He paused and turned his head. He seemed to be reliving the conversation with his wife. Looking back at me, there he was, once again under control. "She said, 'You're free to go to therapy if you want. If you can show me you are finally willing to work on things, then I'll hold off for a month. But you're on your own right now. You've pushed me to the bottom of your priority list for too long.' So, Dr. Stella, I'm here against my will."

"You seem rather calm about all of this."

Grant smiled. "That's the lawyer training kicking in." He rubbed his forehead with his hand and sighed. "The truth is I'm a wreck. I'm not sleeping well. I'm overeating, and I feel like my world is about to spin out of control. In fact, it is out of control. It's just that only Renee and I know it. I really need help dealing with my anxiety and figuring out a way to handle this. I'm about to lose everything."

Step Two: Identify Your Triggers

I asked Grant to tell me more about his background, but unlike most of my clients, he shook his head.

"I'm here to talk about my marriage in the here and now, not go back into the past." For the first time, his face revealed the true feeling of sadness. I could also see a touch of fear.

"Tell me why you don't want to talk about your childhood or family."

"Things happened to me that I don't want to dredge up. I'm stressed out enough as it is. I'm afraid if I talk about the past, I will completely fall apart. My sister went to therapy to deal with things that happened, and she just got worse. The more she talked about her past, the more depressed she got. Eventually, she went to a hospital until she could regain her balance. I don't want that to happen to me."

The pretense of strength was gone. In front of me sat a little boy. He was terrified of what might happen if the truth was told. The idea alone triggered him. I watched as Grant fell into a fear trap.

"I am here to support and help you, not terrorize you," I assured him. "Some therapists used to encourage their clients to repeatedly talk about past abuse with the idea that facing it would lessen its hold. But now we have brain research that explains why some people didn't get better."

"In my sister's case, she got worse."

"Yes, that happens. But that's not the way I work." I explained to him how the brain remembers trauma and how he would learn concrete ways to create pathways around those memories rather than plunge into the dark emotions. He visibly relaxed.

"Okay, let's see how it goes." He took a deep breath. "My parents were both raised in middle class families who have worked hard for where they are in life. My father took it up a notch and is highly influential in this town. Appearances have always been important." He said he and his older sister, Anna, had anything they could want—the best schools, the current fashions, trips abroad—but there was a rigid expectation to bring only honor to the family.

"Anna rebelled against the pressure and eloped on her eighteenth birthday with a young man from an 'inferior' family. She was cut off— emotionally and financially. Our parents told me I had to choose between her or them. I was in high school. What was I supposed to do? Afraid they might throw me out, I cut off contact with Anna. I've never made things right with my sister. That's something I still regret."

"Is that what sent her over the edge?"

"She was completely lost when my parents rejected her. It was like she became a child unable to care for herself. She and her husband were so young and immature. She started drinking and spiraled. She's had a terrible life."

I nodded. "I can see that is painful for you. What came next in your life? How did you meet Renee?"

"In law school. I was attracted to her immediately. She was petite with a radiant smile. Homecoming queen in high school. She even won some local beauty pageants. We started dating right away. But I made sure my parents fully approved of Renee before I asked her to marry me. I thought if I pleased my parents, everything would work out. We got married soon after we graduated.

"I went into corporate law, and Renee went into a family practice. We did very well for ourselves. We bought a big house, drove nice cars, and joined the country club. We were perfectly matched. I would surprise Renee with weekend getaways or nice dinners. I used to send her flowers regularly. But then we decided to start a family, and things became more complicated.

"Renee planned on going back to work after our son's birth, but she discovered she really loved being a stay-at-home mom. We agreed she would leave her job, and as far as I can tell, she never looked back. By our early thirties, we had our second child—a little girl. I felt the need to work extra hours to maintain our lifestyle since we had become a one-income family. Plus my father was pressuring me to move into politics. That's when Renee started complaining about how I was never home."

"What did you do when she expressed her unhappiness?"

"I'll admit I didn't pay much attention to her because, from my point of view, we were the perfect family."

I interrupted. "Perfection is a theme for you?"

"I've always been an overachiever and set extremely high goals for myself," he said. "Renee is gorgeous. I'm always so proud to be with her in public. Plus she is an amazing mother, and our children thrive. I've done all I can to keep the money coming in, but the romantic getaways have fallen by the wayside."

He gazed out the window again. "As I say this out loud, I sound pretty selfish. But it was so much easier to focus on my career than on the marriage. It just felt too hard to make her happy, so I went where the accolades were, I suppose. Getting a sitter for the weekend so we could go out seemed more trouble than it was worth, and my parents, when they're in town, are not the babysitting kind. The more she has tried to get my attention, the more I have resisted. In fact, I sometimes have gotten so irritated that I've done the opposite of what she asked. I didn't want to be nagged, and it felt like all she did was complain."

He paused before continuing. "Renee and I used to want the same things out of life. But now we don't seem to be on the same page. She even asked me if I was having an affair. 'When would I have time for an affair?' I asked her. 'I have always been faithful to you.'

"After she asked me that question, I knew I was in hot water. So I sent her flowers a few times and took her out for a few nice dinners. I even gave her an expensive necklace. She loved it and wore it constantly. But then I got swept away with work again. One night, she took off the necklace in front of me, and said, 'You can't buy me off, Grant. I want a real marriage.'"

He looked down at his well-manicured fingers. "I'll tell you something I've not said to anyone before: I feel like such a fake. The thought of losing Renee and daily contact with my children is horrible. But do you know what I'm also afraid of? Having those at my law office find out what's really going on in my life. How can I launch a political bid when I'm in the middle of a divorce?"

Grant looked at me with pain in his eyes. "Ever since Renee told me she wanted me out of her life, I have felt like an emotional train wreck. She's hounded me for such a long time, but now she has gotten very quiet and withdrawn. I realize she has been going to counseling and finding her own way. She's going to leave me behind if I don't figure out how to fix this. I can't even imagine what my father will say. I just don't know what to do. I don't want to go through a divorce."

"Does it remind you of something in your past?"

Grant looked down. "I've always tried to win my parents' approval, especially my dad's. My whole childhood was based on achievement and looking good. My sister and I were never allowed outside the house unless we were dressed in our finest. Even going grocery shopping, we had to keep up appearances. My mother would say, 'Every book is judged by its cover.'

"My father was especially hard on me growing up. He wanted me to excel in everything, and if I didn't, he'd beat me with a belt. My mother did nothing. So, believe me, I was a good student. I'd do anything to avoid getting the belt.

"My dad's really tall. He was a basketball star in high school. In fact, he went to college on a sports scholarship. I'm sure you noticed that I'm a bit on the short side."

I hadn't, but now that Grant pointed it out, I could see that he'd have had trouble on a basketball court.

He continued. "But he wanted me to make varsity basketball like he had, and, to be honest, I was a great shot. He and I practiced a lot in our backyard, but I hated every minute of it because it simply wasn't my game.

"Until—" Grant smiled. "that one summer when I grew. I was fifteen, and it was quite painful to grow that fast. When I went back to school the next fall, I was certain I'd finally make the team."

"Did you?"

"Nope. All the other guys grew that summer too. I was taller than before, but some of the other guys had hit six feet. I realized I'd never make my dad happy."

"How did you handle that?"

"I yelled at the coach and said I would never try out for his stupid team again, along with a few choice expletives. By the time I got home, the coach had called my dad and told him I'd cussed him out. My dad was in a rage. He dragged me to the driveway for a one-on-one match. I missed a shot, and he slapped me hard in the back of my head. I fell down, dazed for a minute. Something in me snapped. When I stood up, I was furious. My rage pulled me into a cold, clear mental state.

"From then on, I was on fire. Dad didn't realize how much of an advantage I had gotten from my growth spurt. I was all over him. He couldn't make a shot. When the ball bounced off the rim, I jumped over him and slammed it through the net. I shut him down. In fact, I humiliated him. He slammed the ball into the pavement, and it bounced over the wall into our neighbor's yard. He didn't say anything, just stormed into the house. He never played basketball with me again. He never hit me again either."

Grant's First Trigger: Being Faced with His Own Imperfections

Grant was taught by his parents to hold himself to superhuman standards. He learned that anything less than perfection is unacceptable and should be eliminated or hidden—that he must be the best, or he would be worthless. Grant had been deeply scarred by the physical abuse and emotional neglect he suffered. As a result, he had never learned how to accept himself as a human being like everyone else with normal flaws and strengths.

Just Because We Feel It, That Doesn't Mean It's True

Our thoughts and feelings do not always tell us the truth. For example, when my daughter was five years old, she was convinced there was a monster who would reside beneath her bed each evening under the cloak of darkness. It didn't matter what I said or how thoroughly I checked beneath the bed; she believed the monster was there.

Truly terrified, she would sleep with her lights on to prevent the monster from moving out of his hiding place. The strength of her fear led her to believe that the monster was real. As adults, we know that monsters under the bed do not exist. However, we are much like children in that we believe what we are afraid of is automatically real.

You may feel like a monster of failure is lurking to humiliate you, but it isn't. We all make mistakes, succeed at times, and fail at others. Each failure is a learning opportunity. When you start to fear the monster under your bed—or wherever it may be hiding—remember that these are the thoughts of a child, not an adult. Children are terrified of monsters that don't actually exist. When you are trapped by fear, you may think and act like a child. But the monster will disappear like magic once you are out of the fear trap and in touch with yourself in the present. Freedom comes when you own who you are—the adult in the room.

Grant tried desperately to gain his parents' love by becoming a perfectionist. This spilled over into all areas of his life. He didn't just want to have a good marriage; he wanted a perfect marriage. He didn't just want to have happy children; he wanted trophy children. He didn't just want a good career; he wanted a career that would put him in the spotlight. He internalized his parents' message: only perfection would make him worthy.

The little boy inside of him still needed his parents' love and approval. He hoped that if he ran for office, his father would finally give that to him. Grant had been so focused on that goal that he'd shut his eyes to the problems developing in his marriage.

He was overwhelmed by feelings of failure. He never felt loved by his parents. He was alienated from his sister, and Renee—the one person he thought he could count on—was threatening to leave him too. Rather than deal with the situation like the adult he was, Grant was transported back in time to when he was a little boy feeling the sting of his father's belt for not being good enough.

Grant's Second Trigger: The Threat of Public Shame

Grant's parents raised him to believe public shame was the worst possible travesty—even disowning their own daughter for it. If news of his failed marriage came out, Grant anticipated further rejection from his father, friends, and colleagues.

"I don't understand how Renee is willing to disrupt our entire lives for her own selfish needs," he fumed. "We've got investments together, a very public social life, and I have a high-profile job in the area. Doesn't she realize a public divorce would be as humiliating for her as it would be for me?"

Grant's core wound was the fear of being shamed and abandoned when he didn't succeed. Because he secretly felt "less than," he could not find a safe and satisfying place to belong without others' approval. In quiet moments, when Grant wasn't rushing around with work and obligations, an excruciating pain would set in. He told me, "In certain moments, I am so afraid I will fall into a hole and disappear. The only way I can deal with this is to keep busy." Lacking a sense of security, Grant fluctuated between self-loathing and blaming others for his problems.

Step Three: Describe Patterns of Self-Sabotage

Grant grew up in a family that had all the trappings of perfection, along-side secrets no one was supposed to share. Subsequently, he developed highly dysfunctional patterns for dealing with the deep sense of shame he felt. He knew if he ever publicly embarrassed the family like his sister had, he would be discarded by his parents as well. Grant was also aware that his compliance in rejecting his sister contributed to her pain. He was afraid that he was becoming more like his father every day.

Self-Sabotage Pattern One: Hiding Behind a Façade of Perfectionism

Throwing his arms up in the air, Grant said, "I just need to admit it: I'm a fake! I'm never happy for long. Nothing I do seems to be enough." The moments of success relieved his sense of self-doubt, but as soon as the congratulations were over, he fell back into an abyss of pain. His obsession with pleasing others quickly became a quest for perfectionism which was doomed from the start.

No one is perfect; we can destroy our lives trying to be. When we can't achieve perfection, another strategy is to pretend.

No one is perfect; we will destroy our lives trying to be. When we can't achieve perfection, another strategy is to pretend. Grant did both. To mask any sign of weakness, he went to great lengths to create a public image based on pretense rather than sub-stance. When his wife tried to talk to him about issues in their marriage, Grant felt she was saying he was a failure as a husband. He never actually asked her if that's what she thought; he assumed he knew what she was thinking. This was problematic because to Grant, perfect marriages did not have problems. But in reality, all marriages have challenges and must be nurtured to stay healthy.

When Renee finally drew a line in the sand, he acted completely surprised—he had hidden the truth even from himself. He was at the mercy of his amygdala, which told him his marriage was either perfect or a failure, all good or all bad, something to be proud of or horribly ashamed of—no middle ground. As a result, he neglected his family, and now things were unraveling rapidly.

Self-Sabotage Pattern Two: Justifying His Behavior by Criticizing Others

The façade started to crack when Renee accused him of infidelity. All the shame he had felt over his lifetime was triggered at that moment. He was unable to sit down and talk things through. In his mind, Renee became his oppressor—like the opponent he had faced so many times in the courtroom. The rage he felt toward Renee came gushing out in our session with statements like:

- "Does she think she's so special that she could find another man who's better to her than I am?"
- "I have never gone out on her, even though she's nagged and pressured me."
- "Who else would put up with her?"
- "I should just let her go and wait for her to come back, begging to reconcile."
- "Why am I even here in therapy? I've got nothing to be sorry for. She's the one with the problems."

By blaming Renee, Grant gave her all of his power. She was the adult, and he was the little boy. He fell further into the grips of the fear trap of failure.

Step Four: Imagine the Worst-Case Scenario

Because people link their fear of failure with the fear of survival, I asked Grant what he hoped would come of our therapy session.

"I want you to tell me how to fix this."

"Well, let me ask you some questions."

"Ah, now you've become the attorney."

"What would happen if I didn't tell you how to fix this?"

He looked a bit stunned. "That's your job, isn't it?"

I shook my head no. "It's my job to help you figure out what you're willing to do to change yourself, not the situation."

"Well, that's disappointing."

"We can only change ourselves, but I am confident that you have the power to make significant changes. When we change, there's hope for whatever situation we may be in."

He remained defiant. "I'm not the problem."

"Maybe not, but what could happen if Renee files for divorce?"

He became dramatic. "My political aspirations would be ruined. She would publicly humiliate me. I'd lose access to my children. My father would be furious about it. I'd lose everything."

"Let's start with your father. What would happen if your dad was angry?"

"He's angry a lot, actually. I have never lived up to his expectations. So I guess I'd just endure his disappointment again."

"When you were a little boy, you were dependent on your parents for survival," I explained. "If they refused to accept you, in the literal sense, the neglect could be life-threatening. So it makes sense that your immediate reaction to your father's anger would be intense fear. But as an adult, can you survive your father's criticism?"

"I don't need his approval to take care of myself financially or in any other way. I see what you're saying. Dealing with his disappointment and criticism would be emotionally painful but not life-threatening—is that what you're getting at?"

"That's exactly my point."

He shrugged. "It might even be a relief."

"Okay, how would a divorce impact your position in the law firm?"

"So many attorneys go through divorce. It's a stressful job. In fact, one of our leading partners is on wife number four."

"So your law career could survive a divorce."

"Yes, but it's not ideal."

I nodded. "Not ideal but survivable?"

"Okay, yes. I'd survive."

"What else would happen if you got a divorce?"

"I'd miss my kids. That would be horrible. I try to be home in time to kiss them goodnight."

I acknowledged it would be painful for him and his children.

"Divorce is always hard on the children," he said sadly.

"But you would survive, and they would survive. And what about losing Renee?"

"I would hate that. She used to be my strongest supporter."

"But, again, you would survive."

"Yes."

I sat back. "I'd like you to notice how you're feeling right now."

He thought for a moment. "Well, I'm really sad but unexpectedly calm about it all."

"What does Renee want from you?"

"She wants me to admit this is all my fault."

I leaned back. "Are you saying she accepts none of the blame for your marriage?"

"Well, you're right. She doesn't blame me for everything. She wants me to admit I'm not perfect."

"Are you perfect?"

"Of course not."

"Does Renee know you're not perfect?"

"Yes."

"And she stayed married to you knowing that, right?"

Grant sighed. "She just wants me to work on the marriage and stop running away."

"What would happen if you worked on the marriage?"

"I'd have to accept the fact that I'm not perfect," he admitted.

"So you have the choice between humility and humiliation?"

"That's an interesting way to look at it."

I smiled. "You have a great deal of power in this situation. You can stay the course, hide behind your façade, probably lose your marriage, but ultimately be okay. Or you can get honest with yourself and possibly save your marriage. No matter how it turns out, you will survive. What are you going to do?"

He sat back and watched a cloud slowly moving across the distant sky. "If your method helps me save my marriage, then I may keep coming back to work with you."

I must have looked a bit surprised, because he smiled. "Well, we both know I have father issues. I may be ready to take on the core emotional wound in the future—if I can be brave enough."

That put a smile on my face. "Your brain will become more courageous as you work through the process. I have complete confidence in you."

Step Five: Create a Courageous Brain

Grant no longer wanted to be at the mercy of his amygdala. He wanted to believe that he would be okay no matter what happened in his marriage, his career, or his life. And so he had decisions to make. He recognized that perfectionism was a setup for failure because everyone makes mistakes—even Grant. Our best efforts will always be lacking. Therefore, we often pin our sense of well-being on the approval of others, who could at any time declare us worthless. The prospect of failing can be devastating for people who lack a secure sense of self-worth.

We must accept ourselves, flaws and all, if we are going to be free of people-pleasing and the threat of shame.

The change must occur within ourselves. We must accept ourselves, flaws and all, if we are going to be free of people-pleasing and the threat of shame. When humbled by the fear trap of failure, Grant had two choices: to allow his shame to beat him up or to accept his imperfections as a normal human being. Working with Grant was a challenge. His fear of not being the best was so entrenched that he resisted the idea of being good enough. So he committed to engaging in the following focused meditation every morning before he left for work.

Focused Meditation Exercise:

This fifteen-minute meditation is designed to give you freedom from the fear of failure. As you practice this, you will strengthen the pathways in your brain that acknowledge and affirm your strengths. You'll strengthen your self-acceptance as old reflexes of self-condemnation lose their power.

Escape the Fear Trap of Failure
Begin

Get into a comfortable position with your arms and legs uncrossed. Breathe in through your nose and exhale through your mouth. Pay attention to how your body feels as you inhale slowly and then exhale slowly.

Choose one point of focus on your body as you breathe. You might focus on the tip of your nose and the sensation of air moving in and out. You might focus on how your chest rises and falls with each breath. The expansion of your stomach could be another point of focus.

Once you've chosen one part of your body, hold your attention in that place. Continue to breathe slowly in and out. In and out.

If you notice your mind is wandering from your focal point, gently bring your attention back. Let any anxious thoughts drift away. Release any stress you have. You are exactly where you ought to be, doing exactly what you and your body need.

5-Minute Mark

Today we will address the inner critic most of us have inside our heads and begin shifting from the inner critic to a place of gratitude. With the awful things we say to ourselves, it's hard to feel like we're good enough. You've calmed your mind and body, so your inner critic may be quiet right now. Or it's possible the negativity is still strong despite the fact that you have been meditating.

- From this restful place, ask yourself the question "What do I like about myself?"
- You might answer, "I like the way I care about people," or "I like the color of my hair."

For the next several minutes, repeat this affirmation to yourself.

- On the inhale, ask, "What do I like about myself?"
- On the exhale, answer, "I like [fill in the blank]."

Allow yourself to feel accepted and loved, knowing you have many positive attributes.

- Inhale: "What do I like about myself?"
- Exhale: "I like [fill in the blank]."

Concentrate on this positive trait as you become more and more convinced this is true. If you notice your inner critic is arguing with you, don't engage in the conversation. Simply turn your attention back to your positive affirmation.

8-Minute Mark

It's time to focus on a different positive attribute.

- On the inhale, ask, "What do I like about myself?"
- On the exhale, state, "I like [fill in the blank]."

Select something you do well, a successful moment, or something good you know about yourself. Let that affirmation sink in.

- Inhale: "What do I like about myself?"
- Exhale: "I like [fill in the blank]."

Concentrate on this positive trait as you become more and more convinced that it is true. If you notice your inner critic is arguing with you, don't engage in the conversation. Simply turn your attention back to your positive affirmation.

11-Minute Mark

It's time to focus on gratitude. Research has found that expressing gratitude along with the reason for being grateful has a more significant impact on our sense of happiness than expressing gratitude alone.

- On the inhale, ask, "What am I grateful for?"
- On the exhale, say, "I am grateful because [fill in the blank]." It does not have to be anything big; it can be gratefulness for finding a good parking spot when you were running late.

Repeat the above two more times.

14-Minute Mark

Slowly bring yourself back to the outside world. Take a few more deep breaths.

15-Minute Mark

How do you feel about yourself after this meditation? If you repeat this exercise on a regular basis, your sense of self-esteem will improve. You will also find it easier to redirect your inner critic. When you hear negative things about yourself inside your mind, select one of the affirmations in this meditation and focus on that instead.

The more you repeat this meditation, the stronger the positive neuropathways will become. You will create a new habit in your brain. When you feel badly about yourself, it will become easier for you to realize you are good enough. You can remind yourself that you have control over your inner critic's voice. You don't have to silence this voice—just let it speak and then turn your attention elsewhere. You are now ready to engage with your life newly energized to face whatever comes your way.

Step Six: Live Free of the Fear Trap

As Grant continued his meditation exercises and was able to address his issues without being triggered, he saw that self-acceptance requires humility. Being humble is commonly associated with degradation, loss of dignity, or being unimportant. Inherent in this definition, however, is judgment—that you are better or worse than other people. But when we humble ourselves with kindness and self-acceptance, there is no judgment. Rather, humility is the acceptance of what we do well and what we do not do well. We learn to embrace our strengths and imperfections without being critical of ourselves.

Humility comes from a tender place within us—that spot where our vulnerability is ever present, where we do not feel like a winner or a loser, and where we feel connected to those around us. It is the part of us where we acknowledge what we do well without tripping over our ego. In turn, we accept our imperfections, mistakes, and negative feelings without judging ourselves failures.

Humility also allows us to appreciate the gifts and strengths other people have to offer without holding them to impossibly high standards. In this acceptance, we find true connection with others. We not only accept our own humanity, but we accept each other and the human condition.

When Grant first started therapy, Renee was very suspicious about trusting him again. Over time, however, she saw Grant become more patient, less driven, and much kinder. She decided to give him more time to show her he could change. There have been difficult moments as Grant can still become triggered and launch into old patterns. But the more Grant embraces humility, the more he is able to accept and confront the less-than-perfect parts of himself. He isn't as frightened to listen to Renee explain how she feels. He's much less defensive and more accepting.

Grant asked me for a referral for marriage counseling, and he and Renee started working on their marriage together. Only time will tell if they stay together, but with the tools Grant has now, he has good reason to be hopeful.

Key Points

➥ As children, we needed our parents and caregivers to protect us and show us acceptance and love.

➥ We also needed adult role models to show us how to give unconditional love and deal with disappointment and failure.

➥ Without proper role models, we can grow into adulthood without knowing how to accept ourselves and get the support we need when we fail.

➥ If our shortcomings were met with disapproval or abuse as children, we can experience intense pain in the forms of worthlessness, humiliation, and shame as adults.

➥ One response to shame is to become perfectionistic, which sets us up for failure and intensifies our feelings of inadequacy.

➥ Another response to shame is to hide imperfections and pretend they don't exist. We can try to protect ourselves by creating a false persona of success that isolates us from others.

➥ Feeling like a fake is a common experience for people who do not accept themselves.

➥ When we are in the fear trap of failure, we can define ourselves as failures rather than as someone who tried something and didn't reach the goal.

➥ When we cannot accept our own humanity, strengths and weaknesses, we often judge others too harshly as well.

➥ Even though our brains may have recorded shame-based memories, we have power to sidestep these triggers by creating new neuropathways of self-acceptance and kindness.

➥ Self-acceptance requires a sense of humility—the awareness that we are no better or worse than anyone else.

➥ When we accept ourselves, we are able to celebrate our successes without gloating and learn from our failings without the intensity of shame or humiliation.

☞ Self-acceptance allows us to realistically view our own gifts and failings. As we become more accepting of ourselves, we are more capable of accepting the gifts and failings of others as well.

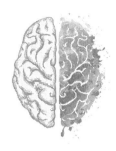

FEAR TRAP SIX

Are You Afraid of the Unknown?

Life shrinks or expands in proportion to one's courage.
—Anais Nin

My first impression of Laura was that of an aging plain Jane. She was of average height, had curly, graying hair, and wore a loose-fitting dress with flats. She was not unattractive, just plain—a person who might go unnoticed in a crowd.

I asked her why she had come to see me.

"My husband, Wayne, died six months ago. He had battled cancer for nearly five years."

"How long were you married?" I asked.

"Forty-two years."

I took in that number. "Wow. I can understand why you'd come here for extra support. That's a huge loss."

To my surprise, she shook her head no. "I'm doing pretty well with that. Wayne and I had great communication. We spent many hours reminiscing over the ups and downs of our life together. And, together, we mourned the future we'd not enjoy together. Before he passed away, both of us had come to accept it."

"So what brought you to therapy?" I was curious.

Her answer was insightful and forthright. "I have lived my life afraid. I have been afraid to drive on the highway, afraid to take a bus across town to visit my sister, afraid to sleep in my house at night alone. I still sleep with a light on. I'm afraid to walk into a room of people I don't know. I'm afraid to go to a movie or a restaurant by myself. I'm afraid to try a different brand of shoes or detergent or shampoo. I could go on and on and on."

Laura took a breath before she continued. "When Wayne was dying, we talked about all the things we could have done but didn't do. We laughed together at this. Wayne was afraid too. He said so. He regretted letting his fears get in the way of doing the things he'd have liked to. His honesty helped me admit the same thing. I don't want to let my fears determine how the rest of my life is lived."

It was with those words that I saw a brave woman, one who wanted to embrace life, who no longer wanted to be ruled by what she was afraid might happen.

Step One: Tell Your Story

I asked Laura about her childhood, and she told me she grew up in a rural area of southern Ohio, between Cincinnati and Huntington, West Virginia. "My father worked as a machinist, and my mother was a home-maker. My extended family lived in the same community, and honestly, I don't remember anyone traveling outside of the area unless it was for military duty. There was a general distrust of 'outsiders.' Even though no one said it out loud, I grew up believing that leaving my hometown would be dangerous and scary. Fear of the outside world was simply a way of life for all of us.

Why It's Hard to Stop Worrying

Did you know that your brain is hardwired to enjoy worrying? It's true. Your amygdala's job is to keep you alive. Part of our body's survival strategy is to reward us when the amygdala does its job effectively. How? By automatically releasing a chemical called dopamine when the amygdala is active.

Dopamine is our pleasure drug. It makes us happy; consequently, we tend to repeat the behaviors that produce this chemical. You and I know that worry can be destructive to our bodies and quality of life—well, we know it in our frontal lobes. But because survival itself is more important than the quality of our survival, the body rewards our amygdala for being active. It doesn't give the same support for reasonable processes in our frontal lobes.

We have a natural reluctance to stop worrying because of the added pleasure we receive from dopamine. Yet the amygdala often ends up triggered when there is no authentic danger at all. It cannot distinguish between a threat that is real or an imagined one. It can be triggered by the fear of running late for work, fear of what someone will think of us, or fear of being chased by a tiger. When we feel like we're in danger—whether we are or not—the amygdala can take over, filling us with worry that is all too often unwarranted. This is what makes it so difficult to stop worrying.

To break free from worry, you'll need to add new layers of neuropathways in your brain. The exercises in this book do exactly that, but they take some time and focus. Remember, our brains respond to repetition, so you have to choose to change. But if you have the will to feel better, you can. It's in your power to overcome these patterns and better manage your triggers.

"Don't get me wrong; it was a good childhood. We didn't have much money, but neither did anyone else I knew. We had plenty of love and were always at each other's homes to eat or hang out."

"How did you meet Wayne?"

She smiled. "Wayne and I grew up together. His family was quite similar. The small group of original settlers in our area included both of our great-grandparents. We followed in their footsteps and were very proud of our little town. In fact, it was quite a scandal when Wayne got a good, stable job at Proctor and Gamble's Ivorydale plant, where Ivory soap was made. After we married, we moved to Cincinnati, seventy-five miles away from our hometown." She giggled at the memory. "We came back home a few times at the beginning, but once we had children, it seemed too dangerous for us to be out on the road. We stayed in touch through letters and phone."

Laura emphasized the next point to be clear. "We were considered the black sheep of our families—me and Wayne. My parents constantly pressured us to move back home, where they said we belonged. At first, I felt guilty and quite afraid of going so far away. But what could we do? There was no work for Wayne back home."

Laura explained that they only had one car, so she stayed in the home most of the time. But soon she became pregnant, and they started their family. After having her first child, Laura no longer felt isolated. She enjoyed being a mother and had five children, each three years apart. Eventually, Laura's sister also moved to Cincinnati but across town. They talked on the phone daily and got to see each other monthly.

She summed up her childhood: "Wayne and I were raised to be afraid and to distrust the outside world. It's as simple as that. No huge childhood trauma. No major tragedy. We were just indoctrinated with a fear of anything or anyone we didn't already know. Even so, Wayne, my sister, and I went further than anyone else in our families."

Laura viewed everything unknown or uncertain through a filter of fear. She was very clear about the fact that she was ready for a change. She declared, "I've always let my fear hold me back. Wayne was the same way. My life has lacked passion. I'm not talking about romantic passion; I mean life passion—adventure. I want to do things I've never done before and see places I've only read about. I want to get out into the thick of life, meet new people, experience new cultures, and have adventures that make my heart race."

Step Two: Identify Your Triggers

"Because Wayne and I had talked so much about our lives together, I was as prepared as possible for his passing. But what I hadn't realized was how empty the house would be without him."

Laura acknowledged that the force of loneliness was prompting her to be more daring. "Last week, I sort of had a panic attack. There was no one to talk to. The place was strangely quiet, almost eerie. I felt so lonely and even a bit afraid to be in the house alone. That's when I decided I wanted to get into therapy. I don't want to live in a constant state of loneliness and fear."

Laura's First Trigger: Feelings of Loneliness and Isolation

I asked Laura about her life before Wayne's death. "I have had a good life. Wayne and I raised five children; they are all on their own, and they no longer need me. I was content in my life as it was until Wayne got sick.

"As Wayne got sicker and sicker, we spent more time watching television. Somehow we got hooked on those traveling shows and documentaries about far-away places. We lived in our Parkview home for almost forty years. It was new when we moved in. Don't get me wrong—I love my home and my family. But at sixty-two years old, all I have ever known is this tiny slice of the world and my role here. There are so many types of people in the world, but everyone we knew was just like us.

"One night after we turned off the TV, Wayne said to me, 'Laura, there's a wonderful, beautiful world out there. I don't have the time but you do. I want you to know that I want you to follow any dream you have. Don't stay in this house for me.'"

She leaned back in her chair and paused, looking out the window. "At first, my grief consumed me. I had no energy to go anywhere and didn't want to leave the house. But after a while, the house was less of a refuge and more of a prison."

Laura realized she missed being able to talk with people face to face. "With Wayne gone, I have no one to talk to—daily. I'm isolated in this little house because I have been too afraid. Sure, I can talk on the phone, but it's not the same thing as being with another person. If I don't overcome my fears, I'll miss out on so much. I miss seeing my children and grandchildren in person and watching them grow up. I want to be part of their lives, not simply a voice over the phone.

"Wayne's words kept coming back to me. He wouldn't have wanted me to stay home trapped in my fear. " She smiled sweetly. "If I were brave enough to travel, I could have a rich and adventurous life—or the remainder of my life. I want more out of my remaining years."

Trigger Two: Encountering the Unfamiliar or Unpredictable

"Being a wife, a mother, and now a grandmother has been wonderful, but I want something more," Laura explained. "Do you know I have only been outside of Ohio once? We went to Oil City, Pennsylvania, for my brother-in-law's funeral. We drove. I have never been on a plane or seen the ocean or mountains besides in pictures and on TV. I have never walked on sand, had a drink in a bar, rode a train, or spent the night in a charming hotel. As a matter of fact, I have only stayed in a hotel twice— first on our honeymoon, and we stayed downtown for two nights, but all we could afford was a Howard Johnson; then in Oil City, and we stayed at an old motel with some name like Eagles Inn."

There are people who live their lives to the fullest. You may know someone enjoying this kind of life. They may not have material wealth, but they are living a life that is meaningful, rich, and full. Their work is not a chore. They are happy. They are not driven by fear.

Too many of us are limited by our fears. We structure our lives to feel safe—to avoid what scares us. In America, we have equated material wealth with security. The unspoken promise says that if we are financially secure, we will be happy. The more we surround ourselves with stuff, the safer we perceive ourselves to be. We consume, store, and waste. But as we know deep down, material or monetary security does not translate into happiness, a sense of confidence, or a life of courage.

Some of us are afraid to leave what is familiar. We resist trying new things. For example, when was the last time you went to a restaurant and tried a dish you've never had before? Familiarity feels comfortable, and comfortable feels safe. We are afraid of risk. In speaking of risk, I am not referring to engaging in dangerous activities that you are not prepared to do. I am referring to our willingness to change—to venture out toward what we really want. When we get outside of our comfort zone, we will feel the fear. But as many of my clients have discovered, fear isn't the real problem. It won't kill you. Fear is quite survivable.

There is absolutely nothing wrong with the desire to feel safe. We all need to be safe. However, an unwillingness to try something unfamiliar keeps us bound by our fear traps.

There is absolutely nothing wrong with the desire to feel safe. We all need to be safe. However, an unwillingness to try something unfamiliar keeps us bound by our fear traps. This prevents us from fully exploring the joy of life.

Step Three: Describe Patterns of Self-Sabotage

Since fear was taught to Wayne and Laura by their families, it's no surprise that once they moved to Cincinnati, they never ventured far beyond their new home. "Neither Wayne nor I thought we could handle the challenges of change or travel," Laura said. "We talked a lot about this together once he fell ill. We had no faith in ourselves. We weren't taught to be self-confident. We avoided anything unpredictable or challenging because that's how everyone in our families lived their lives."

Pattern One: Self-Isolating and Refusing to Try Anything New

Laura and Wayne created a safe life together even though they could have helped each other try new things. Raised to associate the unfamiliar with danger, they constantly reverted back to what they knew.

It was simply easier to keep living her life as she always had. But with Wayne gone and her children moved out, Laura was left alone with her thoughts and her deeply buried longings for more. Each time she felt a longing begin to well, she quickly stifled it. She continuously doused the sparks of passion inside herself.

Laura came to therapy because she realized this was a deeply ingrained pattern of self-sabotage. She continued to lower the quality of her life and relationships in fear of fantastically unlikely scenarios. Yet the loneliness she felt from Wayne's absence became so intense that it motivated her to do something different. She realized that to break through to a more courageous life, she needed extra insight and support.

Pattern Two: Spiraling into Catastrophizing Thoughts

Whenever Laura imagined leaving her house to drive across town, her anxiety stopped her in her tracks. "What if…?" took over her mind as her amygdala was triggered. In terms of negative self-talk, Laura's brain was clouded with catastrophizing thoughts: persistent, intense worry over an extremely unlikely worst-case scenario.

Recent research has shown that approximately ninety-five percent of what we worry about does not happen; this means worry is just a self-defeating waste of emotional energy. Even when Laura began recognizing the fear trap she had fallen into, these extreme possibilities left her paralyzed.

Round and round her thoughts raced as the energy remained trapped in the fear center of her brain. Her amygdala gave her the options to fight, flee, or freeze, and she chose to freeze. In reality, she was an extremely capable woman who had already overcome some of life's greatest challenges.

But her confidence plummeted from the fear that she could easily be overwhelmed by dangerous possibilities outside the front door of her house. Fear of the unknown transformed her back into a small girl, listening to horror stories of the outside world while safely tucked away in her family home.

Step Four: Imagine the Worst-Case Scenario

Laura was a unique client for me. For most of us, one of our worst fears is facing death. Laura had met that challenge head on with Wayne during his illness. Because of the work she had already done with Wayne through his dying process and death, much of Laura's fear of death was resolved. Dying did not seem so frightening. It seemed rather peaceful and merciful. She did, however, have an irrational belief that she might not survive taking any level of risk. Her fear disabled her ability to judge the true level of danger that moving out of her comfort zone might pose.

"Do you realize you and Wayne were astonishingly strong in dealing with life's most difficult challenge?"

When I pointed that out to her, she sat back in surprise. "I guess you're right. I didn't see it that way."

"What are you most afraid of now? It's certainly not losing your husband."

I could tell she wasn't sure. She had to sit back and think a bit. "Well, I'm afraid of nearly everything else: sleeping alone, driving, going out in public, visiting new places."

"So you're a prisoner in your own home." Laura nodded. "If you could do anything today, what would it be?"

"Anything?" Laura asked.

"Yes," I answered.

The idea of doing anything she wanted was enticing. "I'd like to have the courage to visit my sister." Laura said quietly.

"What stops you?"

"I'm embarrassed to say this, but I'm afraid to drive there. Wayne drove me anywhere I needed to go."

"Laura, what is so frightening about driving yourself?"

"I have to take the freeway, and I hate merging into traffic. People drive so fast. Plus it's a thirty-five-minute drive. I could take a bus, I suppose, but I would have to go downtown and transfer. Now that I think of it, it would take a longer time. But what if I drive, and I get scared, and I can't pull over?"

"Why would you need to pull over?"

She looked at me like I should understand. "When it's time to take my exit."

"Let's try an experiment. Imagine what it would be like if you missed your exit."

Laura thought that through. "Well, I guess I would go to the next exit."

"What if you got scared and couldn't pull to the side of the highway?"

"I would panic. When I get like that, I want to be still. I'm not sure what I would do."

"Would you just stop on the highway?"

Laura laughed. "No, I'm not stupid."

I laughed with her. "No, you're not. So what would you do if you panicked?"

She shrugged. "I guess I would keep driving until I could pull over."

"Your fear is a feeling—a terrible feeling but just a feeling. You have the power to decide how you will respond."

"I guess I could practice driving over there when traffic is not bad. I only have to get onto the highway and merge into other traffic once. I think I could do that. It doesn't sound so bad. If I drove on the highway, it

> *When you feel confident in yourself, you realize you can handle unforeseen situations. The unknown becomes less scary and loses its control on your life.*

would be easier to go to activities my grandchildren have. Now I take the long route. I also have AAA if something goes wrong, and they have helped me before."

Again, I asked, "What are you afraid of now?"

"I'm really afraid that I can't deal with stuff, but I know that is not true. I moved away from home when I got married. That was hard, and I did it. I took care of Wayne and helped him die the way he wanted. That was the worst thing, but I did it. I raised five children, and managed our money. I do deal with stuff, even if I don't like it."

I acknowledged that she was quite competent. "Your family taught you to be afraid of things you were able to handle. Though unintentional, this undermined your self-confidence. But you have been very courageous in your life without noticing it. You can do this. I'm certain."

Step Five: Create a Courageous Brain

Laura confronted these fears, realizing that at the heart of these issues was a lack of confidence in her own ability to deal with whatever came her way. "I'm honestly not afraid to die, but going out to dinner with a friend scares me. What's the worst thing that could happen? I might die in a car accident. That would be horrible, but I know I can't let it control my decisions. I've faced the worst—death itself. So the rest of it is quite manageable." Once Laura realized this, she was free to begin carving new pathways of courage over old pathways of fear that kept her from doing what she dreamed of.

Increase Your Sense of Agency

Has anyone ever called you a control freak? Many people try to control situations because the unknown fills them with anxiety. They fear that something dangerous could blindside them, and they lack confidence in their own ability to deal with it. As a result, people who are afraid of the unknown struggle to tolerate the new and unfamiliar because it is unpredictable. A new person, a new place, or even a new meal could trigger someone with this fear.

The primary goal of this book is to increase your sense of agency—your ability to feel in charge of your direction in life. When you feel confident in yourself, you realize you can handle unforeseen situations. The unknown becomes less scary and loses its control on your life.

Focused Meditation Exercise:

The final exercise I want to share with you is different from the others in this book. It will take three days to complete. You will need a small notebook to keep track of your experience. Practicing this will help you evaluate where fear is holding you back and what risks are worth taking.

Escape the Fear Trap of the Unknown
Day One: Worst-Case Scenario

Select a fear that holds you back from how you want to live. On the first day, write in specific detail what you are afraid will happen. Any time a new thought comes to mind, write it down. Be as graphic and as detailed as possible. Capture everything you imagine could go wrong.

Day Two: Benefits

The next day, write in specific detail what you will gain if you face the fear. The more detail you can include, the more longing you will feel for what you could have if you moved beyond your anxiety. What benefits could be yours? How would your relationships improve? How could your health be bolstered? List physical, emotional, relational, spiritual, and any other benefits you can imagine.

Day Three: Cost-Benefit Analysis

On the third day, compare the two lists. What outcomes are more likely to occur? Is the worst-case scenario likely to happen? What could you do to deal with the negative consequences you imagine? Do the possible benefits outweigh the possible negatives? What would be worse: taking the risk or missing your connection with life?

Lastly, make an action plan by utilizing resources to face your fear. Maybe you're not ready to jump into the deep end of your fear. Take small baby steps. Try one tiny change to confront what holds you back. Use any of the meditations in this book that can help your brain find new solutions to outdated reactions.

Ongoing

Make this exercise a regular practice. In one year, schedule a review of your notebook into your calendar. Celebrate your accomplishments. I use this practice each month to keep me moving forward. Select a fear that holds you back from engaging in an activity you have wanted to try. Imagine the worst-case scenario and what you could do if this came true. Would the emotional impact be temporary? The likely answer is yes. Most worst-case scenarios are unlikely and the distress temporary. If you do not face this fear, what will happen? You will be in the same place you are right now. Is that where you want to be?

Step Six: Live Free of the Fear Trap

By creating pathways to courage, Laura caused her life to change. She drove on the highway, visited her sister, and went to movies and restaurants alone. She began to travel, not far but seeing different venues in Ohio and Indiana. In early spring, Laura announced that she and her widowed sister were going to take a road trip. They decided not to plan their route but to follow what felt right.

I did not see Laura again after that visit, but it was not the last time I heard from her. Two weeks after our final appointment, I received a postcard from Kelly's Island. It was followed by one from Detroit, then Chicago, then the Grand Tetons, Yellowstone, Las Vegas, the Grand Canyon, Sedona, Scottsdale (she stayed in a really nice hotel), Palm Beach, San Jose, San Francisco, Portland, Olympia, Seattle, Grand Junction, Denver, Topeka, Columbia, Memphis, Asheville, Wilmington, Atlanta, Tallahassee, Disney World, Miami, Key West, Bonita Springs, Sanibel, Sarasota, Atlanta (again), Hilton Head, Washington DC, Baltimore, New York City, Philadelphia, Buffalo, and Erie, Pennsylvania—a rather circuitous route. The postcards often had a few words—usually "I'm in [the name of a new city]." Occasionally there would be a note after the city such as "ate mussels," "stayed in a five-star hotel," "drove over Bertha's Pass," "felt the snow in the mountains," "saw a play," "walked the glass bridge at the Grand Canyon," "ate bison," "drove across the St. Petersburg/Tampa bridge," "watched the sunrise on the ocean," or "walked around the reflecting pool."

After the last postcard, I didn't hear from Laura for four months. On a Tuesday in late March, I received an envelope with no return address. Inside was a picture of Laura smiling while holding a passport. There was no note, just the photograph. I couldn't help but smile.

Laura was brave. She recognized that the unfamiliar wasn't inherently dangerous—that was a lie she believed when caught in her fear trap. Witnessing her husband's death allowed her to face the ultimate fear that opened the door for her to fully live life. We can all be like Laura. We can sidestep our fear traps by building pathways of courage. This allows us to expand our connection with others and embrace life.

A year after receiving the last envelope with the photograph, I got a note from Laura. She was back home on Parkview Drive—happy, staying put, and enjoying her life with friends. That was the last correspondence I received. I am delighted whenever I think of Laura. She is on a great adventure somewhere in the world.

Key Points

- As children, we needed adults to show us how to take appropriate risks outside of our comfort zones.
- We also needed adult role models to show us how to overcome fear of the unknown and build resilience toward the unpredictable.
- Without proper role models, we can grow into adulthood being afraid to try new things and living small lives within the confines of our fears.
- Unfamiliar or unpredictable situations can trigger us if we have been raised with a deeply ingrained fear of the unknown.
- Negative or frightening experiences that occurred outside of our comfort zones can reinforce the misguided feeling that the entire outside world is dangerous.
- When we are triggered by the unfamiliar, we lose our ability to think realistically about the risk because our amygdala only gives us the options to fight, flee, or freeze.
- Our culture reinforces the idea that material security will make us feel happier and more fulfilled when it truly does not.
- We can overcome the fear of the unknown by comparing the worst-case scenario with the potential benefits to be gained.
- We can also manage our fear of the risks by thinking through what we could do if they did occur.

- ⊶ Even baby steps outside of your comfort zone will move you away from the fear trap of the unknown toward progress, especially when you regularly check back on your goals.
- ⊶ As you gain freedom from this fear trap, you can take steps toward living the life you dream of and discovering your true limits.

Bonus Focused Meditation Exercise

This is the meditation I practice every morning. I can personally attest to its power to increase courage and a sense of self-confidence.

Start by getting into a comfortable position. Breathe in through your nose and exhale through your mouth. If you have been practicing these focused meditations throughout the book, you will probably find that it's much easier to relax than when you first started out. This final exercise will strengthen your sense of courage and self-confidence as you take on new challenges, free of the cycles that once kept you stuck.

3-Minute Mark

Now that you are more relaxed, imagine three levels of bleachers behind you. On the highest level, imagine the source of all love, healing, and goodness. You might imagine God or some other spiritual teacher or ideal. If you do not believe in God or don't view life from a spiritual perspective, simply imagine the power of love as pure energy. Imagine the warmth and joy of love coming toward you. Bask in that sense of security and well-being.

6-Minute Mark

Imagine the second row of bleachers, lower than the first. On this row sit the people whom you revere and admire in history. They may be saints or prophets, teachers or mentors, authors or musicians—anyone who has influenced you with goodness and inspiration. Place them one by one on the bleacher and allow the love coming from the top to combine with theirs into a larger force of goodness and nurturance. Allow this energy to flow around you, inside of you, and through you.

9-Minute Mark

On the third and lowest bleacher are those people who have loved you but are no longer living. They may be teachers or mentors who helped you along the way. Perhaps these are family members: your parents or grandparents, cousins, or siblings. Add to this row friends who have cared for you in significant ways. Imagine all of their love and affection join with the energy from the top two levels. This love is immense! Allow it to flow all around you and fill your heart with joy.

11-Minute Mark

Next, imagine a row of chairs in front of you filled with people who are alive. These are those who love you, encourage you, nurture you, and show you love. Allow the warmth and love that come from those in the bleachers behind you to flow through you to the people in the first row. Cover them with acceptance and gratitude. Allow your eyes to scan the faces of all these people, and with each breath, say to yourself, "I offer the love that flows through me to you." Take time to feel the energy flow into each person.

13-Minute Mark

In the last stage of this meditation, imagine a second row of chairs filled by people whom you find difficult to love. These are people who are hurtful, untrustworthy, and even dangerous to your well-being. Look at each person and offer the same love you gave to those in the first row. Allow yourself to love them from this safe distance, knowing that no one can hurt you in this focused meditation. One by one, give them love.

As you continue to do this meditation, you will find that over time, you may see those you once disliked or even despised in a new light. Your empathy may grow.

Your compassion may increase. Your negative feelings for them may subside. In fact, you may invite some of those in the back row to move up to the first row of those who currently love and nurture you. The fewer people in that back row indicates that you no longer fear them from within yourself. This is not to imply that moving them up a row makes them safe in the outside world. But as your brain develops more neuropathways, you simply won't fear them like you have in the past.

EPILOGUE

It's been nearly twenty years since that life-shattering day in my garden—the day I finally faced the fact that I'd been horribly betrayed and my marriage was over. I was ill-equipped to handle the situation, but in dealing with this loss, I developed the method to create a courageous brain. Not only did this process soothe the deep childhood wounds in my brain, but the Courageous Brain Process also gave me the tools to deal with the challenges that awaited me soon after.

After my divorce, I was diagnosed with two forms of breast cancer, ten years apart. If you or someone you love has ever heard similar news, you can understand the fear that shot up inside me. Initially triggered by the news, my mind started wandering down those old, self-destructive paths again. I responded with a deep sense of victimization. Why me? Why should I have to go through surgery, radiation, and chemotherapy? And why not just once but twice?

However, because the CBP was already so deeply ingrained in me, my brain was prepared to reroute itself. I was quickly able to bring myself back to the present moment, with all of my adult capabilities. The question "Why me?" quickly turned into "Why *not* me?" Cancer is a disease that strikes people of all ages, genders, and racial backgrounds. I am not unique or special. I am not immune to illness or tragedy.

Let me be clear: if cancer were a gift, I would return it. But as with any crisis, the mushroom cloud came with silver linings. I was showered with love as people reached out to me. The confidence inside of me was strengthened by all those who expressed their care. Yes, I felt incredibly vulnerable, but I remembered that I could handle feeling vulnerable. Of course, I do not want to die, but the idea of it no longer paralyzes me with fear.

The trigger threatened to grip me again when my sister became ill with adult-onset type-I diabetes. My biggest fear in life is losing her—it is even greater than fear for myself. She is the one person who shares the deepest traumas and joys of my childhood. Our relationship connects me to my past.

Yet I know I cannot control her health, and I cannot protect her at her job as a private investigator. Through the CBP, I have accepted this. While the thought of losing her still scares me, I am confident in my own capacity to handle loss. This confidence allows me to enjoy my sister, as well as my daughters and all the other people I love, without fear.

I genuinely hope that you seize the message of this book. Your brain is shaped by the pains of your past, but that does not dictate your future. Live a life without fear. It's your choice. With the discipline of meditative practice, you have the power to create a courageous brain and live a truly courageous life.

REFERENCE GUIDE TO FOCUSED MEDITATION EXERCISES

*Please note that I've separated and reprinted here just the meditation exercises found throughout this book. I hope you find it helpful as you continue to meditate.

Focused Meditation Exercises

Fear Trap One: Escape the Fear Trap of Being Alone

The following is a fifteen-minute exercise. I recommend you read over this exercise first and then set a soft timer to remind yourself to go to the next section. It may take once or twice to get the hang of it, but by working through this meditation on a daily basis, you will have the power to change your brain and create new pathways. You'll be able to recover more quickly from being triggered, and with repetition, you may be able to sidestep the trigger altogether.

Begin

Start by getting into a comfortable position. Breathe in through your nose and exhale through your mouth. You may be breathing shallowly, primarily from your chest. Focus attention on breathing deeply into your abdomen. It may take a while to relax to the point where your stomach expands and retracts with each slow breath. Continue to breathe in through your nose and out through your mouth.

5-Minute Mark

Now that you are more relaxed, think of one person in your life now or in your past who you consider a safe person. It could be a best friend, a child, a spouse, a teacher, or a mentor. It can even be a store clerk with whom you have developed a relationship.

Think of this person as you breathe in and out. After a few more breaths, I want you to imagine an invisible string that connects from your heart to theirs. Experience the connection and the warmth of their presence and acceptance. Let their love permeate your body and mind. (Concept from *The Invisible String* by Patricia Karst, published by Little, Brown Books for Young Readers in 2018.)

7-Minute Mark

Select a second person who is or has been safe for you. Keep the thread connected to the first person and attach another string to the second person. Think of this person and how you feel accepted and loved by them. Again, it can be anyone: someone with whom you work, a relative, or a childhood friend.

Think of both these people as you breathe in and out. Let yourself soak up the love traveling through the strings that connect you with these two safe and loving people. Remember that when you are frightened, it's easy to feel you are alone. You are not alone. There are people in your life who accept you and love you.

9-Minute Mark

Add a third person to your meditation. Think of another person who nurtures you or has nurtured you in the past. Choose someone who fills you with a sense of encouragement and hope.

It can be someone who inspires you to be all you can be, someone who believes in you even when things are difficult. This is a person you can go to when you feel lonely and afraid. Connect a string to them and know they are in your life now or in your memory, forever available to you. Sit with the warmth of these three people.

11-Minute Mark

Maintain the connection between you and these three safe and loving people. Imagine yourself as a fourth person who accepts and loves you. Add yourself to the circle so that now you have four people connected to you by strings. Give yourself the love and acceptance you need and deserve.

On the inhale, say, "I accept myself completely."
On the exhale, say, "I am strong and capable."
Repeat this affirmation.
I accept myself completely.
I am strong and capable.

14-Minute Mark

You have been changed through this meditation. Your brain has been soothed. The fear center of your brain has been deactivated, and your frontal lobe has been stimulated. A new, albeit small, neuropathway has been formed. You will strengthen this pathway every time you do this meditation.

Now wiggle your fingers and toes and slowly bring yourself back to the outside world. Take a few more deep breaths. You are now ready to engage with your life, newly energized to face whatever comes your way.

Meditation Completed

I recommend you do this meditation every day for forty days as it will strengthen the neuropathway and create a new habit in your brain. When you feel alone, it will be easier to soothe yourself and remind yourself you have people in your life who love you. Most importantly, you'll more easily recall that you love yourself and believe in your own strength and resilience.

Fear Trap Two: Escape the Fear Trap of Being Rejected

Before you start this fifteen-minute meditation, select an extremely happy moment when you felt accepted and loved without question. Then choose a memory wherein you experienced a sense of rejection without being triggered in a significant way. Once you have those memories ready in your mind, you can begin.

Begin

Start by getting into a comfortable position with your arms and legs uncrossed. Breathe in through your nose and exhale through your mouth. You may be breathing shallowly, primarily from your chest, but focus your attention on breathing deeply into your abdomen. It may take a while to relax to the point where your stomach expands and retracts with each slow breath. Continue to breathe in through your nose and out through your mouth.

5-Minute Mark

Now that you are more relaxed, think of one experience in your life when you felt accepted and secure. You might have experienced this with a special person, or you may have experienced this in a group by feeling like you belonged. Think of this experience as you breathe in and out.

Use all your senses to describe what you saw, felt, smelled, and heard. Experience it as fully as possible. Sit with this memory and allow yourself to feel at peace, loved, and accepted.

8-Minute Mark

Turn your attention to an experience when you felt slighted or mildly rejected. Again, this experience could involve one or more people. Perhaps you felt singled out or embarrassed among a group of your friends. Use all your senses to describe what you saw, felt, smelled, and heard. Experience it as fully as possible. Sit with this memory and allow yourself to feel uncomfortable and unaccepted.

Don't shy away from it; embrace it fully.

When you notice your negative feelings are fading, you will know that your brain has become desensitized to this memory. Set your timer for the twelve-minute mark. If the feelings continue to be strong, then repeat this meditation tomorrow with the same memory. Continue to use this experience until the intense emotional response fades.

12-Minute Mark

Shift your focus back to the positive memory you chose for this exercise. Return to the place where you felt totally loved and accepted. Make this memory as real as possible. Feel the clothes on your body. Smell the fragrance in the air. If you were eating, recall the taste of the food. Listen to the voices and the laughter. Take in the kindness shown to you.

14-Minute Mark

Now wiggle your fingers and toes and slowly bring yourself back to the present. Take a few more deep breaths. You are now ready to engage in your life with a deeper conviction that you are safe and at peace.

15-Minute Mark

You have been changed through this meditation. While you may not have come to a place where your brain is completely desensitized to this memory, your brain has been soothed. The energy level in the fear center of your brain has decreased, and your frontal lobe has been stimulated.

If this meditation is helpful to you, I recommend you repeat it with memories that increase in emotional intensity. If a memory is too painful or upsetting, it's best to seek out a therapist who can be with you through the process. The goal is to become desensitized, not overwhelmed. When we gain control over our fearful memories, our brains begin rewiring our neuropathways.

Fear Trap Three: Escape the Fear Trap of Confrontation

This fifteen-minute exercise is designed to help you face the fear of confrontation. The more you repeat this exercise, the more quickly your brain will be able to calm down when conflict arises. It will strengthen the part of your brain that thinks critically and empathizes to create win-win situations. Before you start, you'll want to find a comfortable place free of interruptions.

Begin

After you find a comfortable place free of interruptions, take deep breaths through your nose and out your mouth. Scan your body from top to bottom, noting areas where you are holding stress.

You may feel tightness in your neck or shoulders or in your face and jaw. Breathe deeply into these areas and allow yourself to relax. You are safe and competent. There's no need to hold on to stress any longer.

Move down your body to your shoulders and arms, your hands and fingers. Release any tension you find there. Notice the depth of your breath. Is it shallow and quick or deep and slow? Take time to slow down your breathing, and take deeper and deeper breaths until you see your abdomen rising and not your shoulders.

Focus on your midsection. Are you holding stress inside yourself? Do you feel any pain? Focus attention on the back of your body. Is there stress between your shoulder blades? Breathe deeply and allow these muscles to relax. Move down to your middle and lower back. Again, imagine breathing into those muscles and release all tension.

Move to your pelvic area and buttocks. Are you holding tension in those large muscles? Allow your breath to fill up your core to relieve stress and replace it with a sense of competence and personal power.

Move down your thighs, knees, and calves, first focusing on your right leg and then your left leg. Rotate your feet and wiggle your toes to allow the stress to pour out of your body and into the floor.

5-Minute Mark

Today we will focus on grounding you in self-confidence, compassion, and courage. Think about the person you want to talk with about an unresolved issue. We often start at a place of anxiety and imagine the worst that could happen in this type of conversation. Instead, think about the best attributes this person possesses. Find specific things about this person that you respect and enjoy. If this is a particularly toxic relationship, there might be only one or two traits that you respect. Be authentic in the characteristics that you choose.

From this restful place, ask yourself the question, "What do I like about this person?"

You might answer, "I like his work ethic," or "I like the way she cares for children."

For the next several minutes, repeat this affirmation to yourself.

On the inhale, ask, "What do I like about this person?"

On the exhale, state, "I like [fill in the blank]."

Allow yourself to feel positive about this person.

Inhale: "What do I like about this person?"

Exhale: "I like [fill in the blank]."

Concentrate on this positive trait as you become more and more convinced this is true.

If you notice your mind shifting to the things you don't like about this person, gently bring your attention back to the positive. Allow yourself to have empathy for them and assume the best about them.

8-Minute Mark

It's time to focus on taking responsibility for your own side of the relationship. You are in charge of understanding yourself and then helping others understand your thoughts and feelings. If you don't tell them how you feel or what you need, others can't respond. It's not up to them to guess or read your mind.

On the inhale, ask, "What do I want or need from this person?"

On the exhale, answer, "I want or need [fill in the blank]."

Repeat this process and notice that you become more confident with each breath. Repeat this exercise with additional things you need or want from this person. Allow yourself to believe that this person is able to respond positively to your request.

11-Minute Mark

Imagine that you are talking to this person and letting them know what you want or need from them or the situation. Continue to breathe deeply, especially if your mind focuses on the worst-case scenario. Remind yourself that you can take care of yourself, no matter how this person responds.

- On the inhale, affirm to yourself, "I will do my best."
- On the exhale, say, "I am safe and secure no matter the outcome."

Repeat this affirmation while noticing your breath. Has your breathing become shallow, or has it remained deep? As you repeat the affirmation, allow your mind to scan your body and note any places of tension. Allow this affirmation to speak to those areas of stress and bring relaxation and confidence to your entire body.

14-Minute Mark

Slowly bring yourself back to the outside world. Take a few more deep breaths.

15-Minute Mark

How do you feel about yourself and the other person after this meditation? If you repeat this exercise on a regular basis, your sense of confidence to handle conflict will increase. You will also find it easier to talk calmly about your feelings, needs, and concerns. When you feel anxious about having to confront an uncomfortable situation, you will be more equipped to stay true to your feelings, express them with less anger or defensiveness, and be able to cope regardless of the outcome. New pathways will be formed, and it will be easier to assume good faith about the other person. If they do not respond as you hope, you can be confident in your own strength and integrity.

Fear Trap Four: Escape the Fear Trap of Being Ignored

When you feel your needs are not being met, this fourteen-minute exercise reminds you of your own strength and capability. Over time, you will be able to regain your sense of safety, set boundaries to protect your needs, and communicate what you need from those around you.

Begin

Get into a comfortable position with your arms and legs uncrossed. Breathe in through your nose and exhale through your mouth. You may be breathing shallowly, primarily from your chest. Focus your attention on breathing deeply into your abdomen. It may take a while to relax to the point where your stomach expands and retracts with each slow breath. Continue to breathe in through your nose and out through your mouth.

5-Minute Mark

Now that you are more relaxed, imagine yourself, as an adult, sitting in a room with yourself as a child. As this picture comes into your mind, notice what age you are. What are you wearing? What are you feeling?

- As you breathe in, say to the child-self, "You are safe because…"
- On the exhale, say, "I am here with you."
- Repeat this as many times as you choose.
- On the inhale, say, "You are safe because…"
- On the exhale, say, "I protect you."

Repeat this as many times as you choose.

- On the next inhale, say, "You are safe because…"
- On the exhale, say, "I pay attention to your needs."
- Repeat this as many times as you choose.
- On the inhale, say, "You are safe because…"
- On the exhale, say whatever affirmation comes to your mind.

Repeat this as many times as you choose.

For the next few minutes, repeat these assurances or create your own that meet the specific needs of who you were as a child.

As an adult, you can protect your child-self. Allow yourself to feel safe and protected.

10-Minute Mark

Imagine you are in the present moment, and you are talking kindly to yourself. We are replacing the negative self-talk with new affirmations.

- On the inhale, say, "My needs are important because…"
- On the exhale, say, "I am a person of value."
- Repeat this as many times as you choose.
- On the inhale, say, "I make my needs known because…"
- On the exhale, say, "I am an adult who speaks up."

Repeat this as many times as you choose.

- On the inhale, say, "I am safe because…"
- On the exhale, say, "I set boundaries that protect me."
- Repeat this as many times as you choose.

Continue this pattern by filling in the phrases that will strengthen your sense of safety. You are not invisible. You are an important person who deserves to be safe and have your needs met.

14-Minute Mark

It's time to bring your attention to the present moment. Your inner world has been changed through this meditation. Your brain has been soothed. The fear center of your brain has been deactivated, and new neuropathways have been formed. You will strengthen these pathways every time you do this focused meditation.

As you continue this, you will be more able to soothe yourself when you feel invisible or like no one understands you. The more you pay attention to yourself and the more you understand yourself, the more you will be able to share with others what you need. The more you love yourself, the more you will believe in your own worth and value.

Now wiggle your fingers and toes and slowly bring yourself back to the outside world.

Take a few more deep breaths. You are now ready to engage with your life newly energized to be confident and able to speak up for yourself.

Fear Trap Five: Escape the Fear Trap of Failure

This fifteen-minute meditation is designed to give you freedom from the fear of failure. As you practice this, you will strengthen the pathways in your brain that acknowledge and affirm your strengths. You'll strengthen your self-acceptance as old reflexes of self-condemnation lose their power.

Begin

Get into a comfortable position with your arms and legs uncrossed. Breathe in through your nose and exhale through your mouth. Pay attention to how your body feels as you inhale slowly and then exhale slowly.

Choose one point of focus on your body as you breathe. You might focus on the tip of your nose and the sensation of air moving in and out. You might focus on how your chest rises and falls with each breath. The expansion of your stomach could be another point of focus.

Once you've chosen one part of your body, hold your attention in that place. Continue to breathe slowly in and out. In and out.

If you notice your mind is wandering from your focal point, gently bring your attention back. Let any anxious thoughts drift away. Release any stress you have. You are exactly where you ought to be, doing exactly what you and your body need.

5-Minute Mark

Today we will address the inner critic most of us have inside our heads and begin shifting from the inner critic to a place of gratitude. With the awful things we say to ourselves, it's hard to feel like we're good enough. You've calmed your mind and body, so your inner critic may be quiet right now. Or it's possible the negativity is still strong despite the fact that you have been meditating.

From this restful place, ask yourself the question "What do I like about myself?"

You might answer, "I like the way I care about people," or "I like the color of my hair."

For the next several minutes, repeat this affirmation to yourself.

On the inhale, ask, "What do I like about myself?"

On the exhale, say, "I like [fill in the blank]."

Allow yourself to feel accepted and loved, knowing you have many positive attributes.

Inhale: "What do I like about myself?"

Exhale: "I like [fill in the blank]."

Concentrate on this positive trait as you become more and more convinced this is true. If you notice your inner critic is arguing with you, don't engage in the conversation. Simply turn your attention back to your positive affirmation.

8-Minute Mark

It's time to focus on a different positive attribute.

On the inhale, ask, "What do I like about myself?"

On the exhale, state, "I like [fill in the blank]."

Select something you do well, a successful moment, or something good you know about yourself. Let that affirmation sink in.

Inhale: "What do I like about myself?"

Exhale: "I like [fill in the blank]."

Concentrate on this positive trait as you become more and more convinced that it is true. If you notice your inner critic is arguing with you, don't engage in the conversation. Simply turn your attention back to your positive affirmation.

11-Minute Mark

It's time to focus on gratitude. Research has found that expressing gratitude along with the reason for being grateful has a more significant impact on our sense of happiness than expressing gratitude alone.

On the inhale, ask, "What am I grateful for?"

On the exhale, say, "I am grateful because [fill in the blank]." It does not have to be anything big; it can be gratefulness for finding a good parking spot when you were running late.

Repeat the above two more times.

14-Minute Mark

Slowly bring yourself back to the outside world. Take a few more deep breaths.

15-Minute Mark

How do you feel about yourself after this meditation? If you repeat this exercise on a regular basis, your sense of self-esteem will improve. You will also find it easier to redirect your inner critic. When you hear negative things about yourself inside your mind, select one of the affirmations in this meditation and focus on that instead.

The more you repeat this meditation, the stronger the positive neuropathways will become. You will create a new habit in your brain. When you feel badly about yourself, it will become easier for you to realize you are good enough. You can remind yourself that you have control over your inner critic's voice. You don't have to silence this voice—just let it speak and then turn your attention elsewhere. You are now ready to engage with your life, newly energized to face whatever comes your way.

Fear Trap Six: Escape the Fear Trap of the Unknown

The final exercise I want to share with you is different from the others in this book. It will take three days to complete. You will need a small notebook to keep track of your experience. Practicing this will help you evaluate where fear is holding you back and what risks are worth taking.

Day One: Worst-Case Scenario

Select a fear that holds you back from how you want to live. On the first day, write in specific detail what you are afraid will happen. Any time a new thought comes to mind, write it down. Be as graphic and as detailed as possible. Capture everything you imagine could go wrong.

Day Two: Benefits

The next day, write in specific detail what you will gain if you face the fear. The more detail you can include, the more longing you will feel for what you could have if you moved beyond your anxiety. What benefits could be yours? How would your relationships improve? How could your health be bolstered? List physical, emotional, relational, spiritual, and any other benefits you can imagine.

Day Three: Cost-Benefit Analysis

On the third day, compare the two lists. What outcomes are more likely to occur? Is the worst-case scenario likely to happen? What could you do to deal with the negative consequences you imagine? Do the possible benefits outweigh the possible negatives? What would be worse: taking the risk or missing your connection with life?

Lastly, make an action plan by utilizing resources to face your fear. Maybe you're not ready to jump into the deep end of your fear. Take small baby steps. Try one tiny change to confront what holds you back. Use any of the meditations in this book that can help your brain find new solutions to outdated reactions.

Ongoing

Make this exercise a regular practice. In one year, schedule a review of your notebook into your calendar. Celebrate your accomplishments. I use this practice each month to keep me moving forward. Select a fear that holds you back from engaging in an activity you have wanted to try. Imagine the worst-case scenario and what you could do if this came true. Would the emotional impact be temporary? The likely answer is yes. Most worst-case scenarios are unlikely and the distress temporary. If you do not face this fear, what will happen? You will be in the same place you are right now. Is that where you want to be?

Bonus Focused Meditation Exercise

This is the meditation I practice every morning. I can personally attest to its power to increase courage and a sense of self-confidence.

Start by getting into a comfortable position. Breathe in through your nose and exhale through your mouth. If you have been practicing these focused meditations throughout the book, you will probably find that it's much easier to relax than when you first started out. This final exercise will strengthen your sense of courage and self-confidence as you take on new challenges, free of the cycles that once kept you stuck.

3-Minute Mark

Now that you are more relaxed, imagine three levels of bleachers behind you. On the highest level, imagine the source of all love, healing, and goodness. You might imagine God or some other spiritual teacher or ideal. If you do not believe in God or don't view life from a spiritual perspective, simply imagine the power of love as pure energy. Imagine the warmth and joy of love coming toward you. Bask in that sense of security and well-being.

6-Minute Mark

Imagine the second row of bleachers, lower than the first. On this row sit the people whom you revere and admire in history. They may be saints or prophets, teachers or mentors, authors or musicians—anyone who has influenced you with goodness and inspiration. Place them one by one on the bleacher and allow the love coming from the top to combine with theirs into a larger force of goodness and nurturance. Allow this energy to flow around you, inside of you, and through you.

9-Minute Mark

On the third and lowest bleacher are those people who have loved you but are no longer living. They may be teachers or mentors who helped you along the way. Perhaps these are family members: your parents or grandparents, cousins, or siblings. Add to this row friends who have cared for you in significant ways. Imagine all of their love and affection join with the energy from the top two levels. This love is immense! Allow it to flow all around you and fill your heart with joy.

11-Minute Mark

Next, imagine a row of chairs in front of you filled with people who are alive. These are those who love you, encourage you, nurture you, and show you love. Allow the warmth and love that come from those in the bleachers behind you to flow through you to the people in the first row. Cover them with acceptance and gratitude. Allow your eyes to scan the faces of all these people, and with each breath, say to yourself, "I offer the love that flows through me to you." Take time to feel the energy flow into each person.

13-Minute Mark

In the last stage of this meditation, imagine a second row of chairs filled by people whom you find difficult to love. These are people who are hurtful, untrustworthy, and even dangerous to your well-being. Look at each person and offer the same love you gave to those in the first row. Allow yourself to love them from this safe distance, knowing that no one can hurt you in this focused meditation. One by one, give them love.

As you continue to do this meditation, you will find that over time, you may see those you once disliked or even despised in a new light. Your empathy may grow. Your compassion may increase. Your negative feelings for them may subside. In fact, you may invite some of those in the back row to move up to the first row of those who currently love and nurture you. The fewer people in that back row indicates that you no longer fear them from within yourself. This is not to imply that moving them up a row makes them safe in the outside world. But as your brain develops more neuropathways, you simply won't fear them like you have in the past.

ACKNOWLEDGMENTS

Writing this book was an adventure that many took with me, especially since it's my first one. First, I want to thank my daughters, Liz and Maria, for your unconditional encouragement and your unending Starbucks runs.

Next, I want to thank David Forrester for creating the Matrix, which provided the foundation for the Courageous Brain Process. Without your generosity and support, this book wouldn't have come into existence.

I want to also thank my many clients who shared their fears, struggles, and triumphs with me. You are more courageous than you probably recognize, and I am honored to have been part of your journeys.

The team at Berry Powell Press was delightful to work with. I want to thank Carmen Berry for seeing the vision in my first draft, and the assistance to strengthen it. My gratitude includes Carolyn Rafferty for her video expertise. No book is complete without editing, and I am grateful to Abigail Dengler, Valeri Barnes, Marianne Croonquist, Kathleen Taylor, Ashley Jones, copyeditor Doreen Michleski, and proofreaders Bret Workman and Coleen Hanna, PhD for making this all happen. I must also thank Becky Rickett for designing a beautiful cover and my website as well. I am grateful to Roy M. Carlisle for consulting on the entire project.

Lastly, I want to thank Moca, Enzo, and Frankie for keeping my feet warm as I worked on my computer.

ABOUT THE AUTHOR

Nancy Stella, Ph.D., Psy.D. has been a leading clinical psychologist in the Cincinnati area for over twenty years. As former President and owner, Dr. Stella expanded BridgePointe Psychological and Counseling Center into one of Ohio's largest private, multispecialty mental health practices with over seventy-five providers.

After a shattering divorce, Dr. Stella found traditional therapeutic approaches wanting, and developed the Courageous Brain Process (CBP), an innovative, science-based method of therapy. Rooted in the most up-to-date neuroscience, it bypassed the shortcomings of traditional talk therapy to repattern the way our brains process fear.

When the results proved to be undeniably effective, Dr. Stella left BridgePointe in 2014 to open a counseling practice focused solely on CBP. As a result, countless clients have been able to break free of self-destructive patterns triggered by unresolved fear. In addition, Dr. Stella provides training and consultation to other clinicians who want to include this method in their practices.

Nancy Stella holds two doctorates—a PhD in social psychology, and a PsyD in clinical psychology. She is the recipient of the American Psychological Association Monetary Award for her dissertation presentation in Toronto, and the First Phoenix Award from the Cincinnati Academy of Professional Psychology. She has sat on multiple professional

Nancy Stella PhD, PsyD

and community boards, and has served as both the President and Ethics Chair of Cincinnati Academy of Professional Psychology. Dr. Stella has donated time to community organizations including Hospice of Cincinnati, Inter-Faith Hospitality Network, Meals on Wheels, Children's Hospital, and Shriner's Hospital.

Dr. Stella lives in Cincinnati, OH with her three dogs and, for fun, she is currently learning Italian.

To connect with Dr. Stella, please visit her website at:
www.NancyStella.com
For more information on ordering books, please visit:
Berry Powell Press at www.berrypowellpress.com